GhostHunter Walks in Dorset

Rupert Matthews

S.B. Publications

First published in 2004 by S. B. Publications
19 Grove Road, Seaford, East Sussex BN25 1TP
Tel: 01323 893498
Email: sbpublications@tiscali.co.uk

Legio II Augusta may be contacted through their website: www.legiiavg.org.uk

ISBN 1-85770-294-8

Designed and Typeset by EH Graphics (01273) 515527

Front cover photo: Coast path, Lyme Regis
Back cover photo: Ruined church of Knowlton

Contents

*The author stands on the Cobb with the haunted harbour
of Lyme Regis behind him.*

Location of GhostHunter Walks in Dorset

Short Walks under 2 miles
1 - Dorchester
2 - Shaftesbury
3 - Cerne Abbas
4 - Lulworth Cove

Medium Walks under 7 miles
5 - Lyme Regis
6 - Corfe Castle
7 - Maiden Castle
8 - Cull-pepper's Dish
9 - Tarrant Gunville
10 - Horton

Long Walks over 7 miles
11 - Gussage All Saints
12 - Beaminster
13 - Sturminster Newton
14 - Bridport

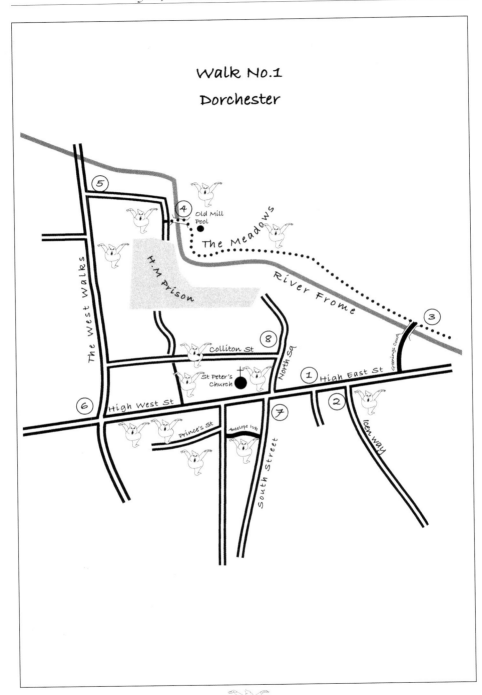

Walk No.1

Dorchester

Dorchester Town Centre

Distance:	**1 mile**
Ghostly Rating:	*** * * * * * * * * * * ***
Route:	**Dorchester town centre**
Map:	**OS Explorer OL15**
Start/ Parking:	**Town centre car park, beside tourist information centre**
Public Transport:	**Dorchester is served by two railway stations and is linked by bus and coach routes to Poole, Weymouth and other towns.**
Conditions:	**A short walk over town streets and pavements. There are no steep hills nor difficult terrain.**
Refreshments:	**There are numerous pubs, cafes and restaurants in Dorchester to suit most tastes and pockets.**

Dorchester is a county town of great character. It is, of course, at the centre of "Hardy Country" and as such has numerous reminders of the great writer, Thomas Hardy. More than one of his novels was set here, though the town was fictionalised as 'Casterbridge' and short stories and poems also relate to this town. People have lived here for over 5,000 years, so it is no surprise that ghosts are thick on the ground.

The Walk

1) Park in one of the town centre car parks, there are several, and make your way to the King's Arms in High East Street.

This is just one of the many welcoming pubs, cafes and restaurants in Dorchester which offer refreshment of various kinds and to suit most pockets. The King's Arms also features in one of Hardy's novels. It was here that the Mayor of Casterbridge, in the novel of that name, held his grand banquet.

The stone house of Icen Way, built using masonry from the former prison. The area is still troubled by ghosts of those held here in the most dreadful conditions.

The Meadows, which lie beyond the River Frome, have been haunted by a mysterious grey lady for years.

Standing with your back to the pub, cross the road and turn left to walk down the hill.

2) After about 150 yards the turning Icen Way is on the right, marked by buildings made of stone.

This is the site of the old prison and the stone houses here are built with masonry taken from that institution when it was demolished to be replaced by the Victorian edifice to be met later in this walk. It was from this prison that those condemned to death by Judge Jeffreys were dragged on hurdles along Icen Way to the site of execution on the hill visible at the end of the road. It is said that the horses hooves and sounds of dragging wood can still be heard in this narrow street late at night.

Judge Jeffreys earned himself the name "Bloody Judge" because of the summary and merciless judgment he handed down to the followers of the Duke of Monmouth in 1685. Monmouth, an illegitimate son of King Charles II, was young, dashing, handsome and charming. Unfortunately he was not too intelligent. The rebellion he led against his uncle, King James II, was poorly organised and ended in defeat at the Battle of Sedgemoor in Somerset. Monmouth himself was beheaded in London, and James sent Judge George Jeffreys to hand out severe punishment to those who had followed the hapless young man. Most of Monmouth's support had been drawn from the West Country and the echoes of the doomed rebellion feature strongly among the ghosts of Dorset.

Cross the road again and continue downhill to the narrow entrance to Greenings Court on the left opposite a Chinese take away.

3) Follow this narrow path down to the canal and cross over to turn left along the towpath. The towpath follows the river as it bends sharp right. As you turn the corner the prison stands on the high bluff beyond the river.

The top of this slope was the site of the public gibbet in early Victorian times. The meadows opposite were the venue for great crowds on an execution day and many fair stalls were put up here. The meadows are now the haunt of a grey lady. Some say she is

The ominously silent mill pond below the prison's walls where an escaping prisoner drowned, and returns to recreate his death complete with clanking chains.

Martha Brown, hanged here in 1856 for murder. Others disagree saying she is a much older phantom dating from Tudor days. If she is the luckless Martha Brown, this provides another link to Hardy. He was in the great crowd which gathered on the meadows to watch the hanging and later used the scene in his writings.

At the end of the towpath a deep, silent pond lies on the right.

This is the old drop pool for the watermill that once stood on this site. As you can see it is overgrown and covered in algae. It was just as overgrown one night in the 1880s when a prisoner managed to escape from the prison after months spent gradually unpicking the mortar around the bars in his cell. He was loaded down with chains and a leg iron, but had bribed a blacksmith in the town to remove these for him. The unfortunate man never made it to his blacksmith. As he hurried over the footbridge, he missed his step and stumbled into this deep pool of water and drowned. His ghost lurks here still, and is one of the few that is actually known to clank his chains in the manner popularly believed to characterise ghosts.

The sole remaining column of Dorchester's Roman town house where a grim discovery made during the archaeological excavation may explain the haunting of the site.

4) Cross the bridge and turn right along the side road. A gate in the brick wall on top of the earthen slopes to your left give access to the park in the centre of which lies the excavated Roman House.

Unusually for a Roman site, the mosaics have been left in place instead of being removed to a museum. When the house was excavated the pathetic bones of a baby just a few weeks old were found in the foundations. This grim discovery may explain the plaintive crying that has been heard in this park from time to time. Dorchester was the Roman city of Durnovaria, one of the largest and most prosperous in southern Britain. Unlike some, it survived the English invasions and continued to be a busy centre for the surrounding countryside through the Middle Ages and down to our own times.

5) Retrace your steps out of the gate and turn left. At the road junction turn left again to walk along The West Walks.

This raised path traces the site of the old Roman walls. The dominating position of the steep slopes that drop sheer away to the floodplain of the River Frome made this a naturally strong position. The stone and

The footpath which runs along the old Roman ramparts of Dorchester, and which is now haunted by a phantom over 1,800 years old.

A modern military history enthusiast from the Legio II Augusta stands to attention in the equipment reported to be worn by Dorchester's phantom legionary.

brick walls and bastions that once crowned these heights remained in good repair when the English came, which might explain how Durnovaria managed to escape the bloody fate that overtook so many other Roman cities at this time.

One of the Roman soldiers who guarded the citizens within the walls still patrols his section of wall. He paces slowly along the Walks dressed in typical Roman armour and carrying the oblong shield for which the Romans are known.

6) Follow the Walks to a crossroads. This walk can be combined with Walk 7 - Maiden Castle. Continue straight on at this junction along the B3147 towards Weymouth. About 500 yards along this road lie the prehistoric earthworks of Maumbury Rings, which mark Point 6 on the Maiden Castle Walk. To continue on the town centre walk, turn left into High West Street. On your right is the Wessex Royal Hotel.

This sumptuous hotel has a ghost that is unusual in that it is never seen from within the building, only from outside. Dressed in a long dark dress and wearing a bonnet set at a jaunty angle, this lady ghost stands looking out of one of the ground floor windows. She seems to be scanning the passing crowds for a familiar face, but it never comes. One Blue Badge Guide attached to Dorchester Tourist Information Centre used to take advantage of the fact that this hotel has a pianola situated in the bar. He would stop his group outside the relevant window and retell the story of the ghost while his wife, who worked in the hotel, set the pianola playing. The sight of a piano apparently playing itself was enough to convince several tourists that they were seeing the antics of the ghost.

Further down High West Street is the Judge Jeffreys Restaurant on the right.

It was in this building that Judge Jeffreys stayed while conducting the Bloody Assizes in Dorchester. Jeffreys was a highly skilled and talented lawyer before he became a judge, and was equally adept at playing politics at Court. He had already held a series of lucrative positions when Catholic King James II sent him to the West Country to try those who had followed the rebellion of the Protestant Duke of Monmouth in 1685. Having successfully hanged, whipped or transported the accused, none of whom were given a fair trial and precious few acquitted, Jeffreys returned to London to be given a peerage by James. These excesses began the slide into unpopularity that

Troubled by more than one spectre, the old lodgings of the infamous "Bloody" Judge Jeffreys harbour sombre memories for Dorchester and for Dorset.

Scene of one of the county's best authenticated ghosts, St Peter's Church dominates central Dorchester.

would drive James from his throne in 1688. Monmouth's tragedy was that he knew all about his uncle's failings but he chose to raise rebellion before they had become clear to the mass of the population.

Although Jeffreys obviously had a clear conscience about the judicial killings he perpetrated in Dorchester, the house where he stayed still has echoes of those dreadful days. More than one of his victims has been seen in spectral form to visit this building. The poor phantoms move slowly about the place as if overwhelmed with sadness.

Opposite is St Peter's Church, scene of a well authenticated haunting.

In 1813 the hugely popular Reverend Nathaniel Templeman passed away and was buried in the church he had loved and served with equal fervour during his lifetime. It was not long before stories began to circulate that the phantom of the good rector had been seen in and around the church.

The stories were not taken terribly seriously until Christmas Eve 1814 when the sextons Clerk Hardy and Ambrose Hunt were decorating the church for Christmas. After labouring for some hours, the men finished their task and decided that they deserved something to refresh themselves before going home. Rather than walk over the road to an inn, the men helped themselves to a glass each of communion wine from the vestry. No sooner had Hardy and Hunt sat down on a pew in the nave to drink than they realised they were not alone. Walking up the nave towards them was the phantom of Rev. Templeman. The ghost was clearly angry, shaking his head and working his mouth as if shouting admonitions - though the two men could hear nothing. Hardy fainted at this point, while Hunt fell to his knees and recited the Lord's Prayer. When he opened his eyes, the ghost was moving off towards the Choir, where it vanished. The ghost of the vicar was seen several times after this event, but he has not put in an appearance since the early 20th century. Perhaps he has finally moved on.

Incidentally, Judge Jeffreys ordered that the severed heads of those he sent to the scaffold should be displayed by being spiked on the railings which surround this church. As soon as he had left town to continue his devilish work elsewhere, the good townsfolk of Dorchester took the heads down.

7) Turn right into South Street. On your right is the Antelope, now converted into a shopping arcade but once the largest hotel in Dorchester.

The Devil himself came to Dorchester some years ago.

The archway in Antelope Walk from which the doom-laden ghost of Judge Jeffreys has been seen to emerge.

The phantoms which trouble this building are again linked to the Bloody Assizes of Judge Jeffreys. The large upstairs hall of the Antelope, now a restaurant, doubled as the court room in 17th century Dorchester. It was here that Jeffreys passed sentence on the unfortunates who came before him. The walkway through the arcade follows the covered way through which coaches would pass from the street to the courtyard beyond. In the courtyard a doorway set back into an arch leads to Judge Jeffreys Restaurant. It was out of this door that the judge would walk on his way to court each morning, and back through which he returned each evening. It is here that his ghost walks still. Wearing a long, flowing wig and dressed in a richly embroidered coat, the thin, halting figure of Jeffreys comes out of the door, turns left along the arcade and then right into what was the entrance to the Antelope. Those who have seen him report an air of unease that comes over them at the time. Almost as if the long-dead judge could still menace those who displease him.

Walk up Antelope Walk to reach Trinity Street beyond. In Prince's Street in front of you stood the Old City Hospital before the shiny new hospital was built on the town's southern outskirts in the late 20th century.

The ghost seen here has been reported at many hospitals. This is "the other nurse". She stands at the end of the bed and looks at the patient the night before he dies. The doomed patient will say to his nurse: "Who is that other nurse who visited me tonight? That very ladylike one all in white standing at the foot of the bed?" But of course there is no other nurse. Only the patient can see the white lady. The strange feature of this ghost is that the person seeing it *always* makes a big thing of saying that she is a *lady*. In some hospitals she has a name, but usually not. Here at Dorchester she goes by the name of Nurse Kitty. Whether there ever was a living Nurse Kitty, nobody seems to know. In any case she has not been seen since the old

St Peter's Churchyard features in a poem about Dorset ghosts by the celebrated Dorset novelist, Thomas Hardy.

hospital was converted into flats or redeveloped and she has not been reported in the new hospital.

8) Return to South Street and turn left to cross High West Street into North Square. The first turning on the left is Colliton Street. On the left, part way up, is an old house.

This old house was once visited by a figure that most of us must hope we never meet. The Devil himself came here to tempt John White, the vicar of St Peter's in the 17th century. The terrifying figure appeared in the vicar's bedroom as the man was preparing for bed. Startled and frightened, but still able to think clearly, Rev. White declared "I've better things to do than talk to you". Looking somewhat discomfited, the Devil vanished.

Continue up Colliton St to take the first left. On the left is the churchyard of St Peter's. It was of this spot that Thomas Hardy wrote:

> Its former green is blue and thin
> And its once firm legs sink in and in
> Soon it will break down unaware
> Soon it will break down unaware.
>
> At night when reddest flowers are black
> Those who once sat hereon come back
> Quite a row of them sitting there
> Quite a row of them sitting there.
>
> With them the seat does not break down
> Nor winter freeze them, nor flood drown
> For they are as light as upper air
> They are as light as upper air.

This lane opens back into High West Street. Turn left to walk down the hill to return to the King's Arms.

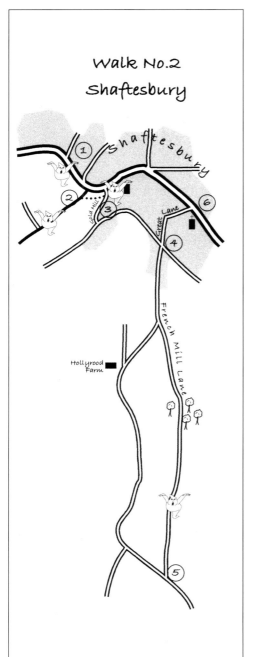

Walk No.2
Shaftesbury

The Gold Hill, famous from television adverts, where a haunting dates back over a thousand years.

The French Mill Lane, just outside Shaftesbury, where some off-duty soldiers had a truly terrifying encounter with the supernatural.

Shaftesbury

Distance:	**1.5 miles or 3.5 miles**
Ghostly Rating:	*** * * ***
Route:	**Shaftesbury**
Map:	**OS Explorer 118**
Start/ Parking:	**Shaftesbury Tourist Information Centre**
Public Transport:	**Shaftesbury is linked by an hourly bus service to the railway at Gillingham and by less frequent bus services to other towns.**
Conditions:	**A short walk through the town centre with two short, steep hills and an optional excursion into the countryside.**
Refreshments:	**Shaftesbury has several pubs, cafes and restaurants to offer refreshments to suit most tastes and budgets.**

Shaftesbury is a delightful old town perched on top of a steep hill. It was founded in Saxon times and survived a Viking attack during the reign of Alfred the Great in the 870s. It was in recognition of this action that Alfred chose Shaftesbury as the site for an abbey when his daughter took holy orders. The Abbey survived for generations, until closed down by Henry VIII in the 16th century. The ghosts of Shaftesbury are mainly linked, one way or another, to the Abbey which dominated the town for so many generations.

The Walk

1) Park in the car park behind the Tourist Information Centre. Leave the car park passing the information centre on your right. This is Bell Street, which meets High Street at a T-junction. Straight ahead is the impressive facade of the Grosvenor Hotel.

The current building is of 17th century date and features in the novel *Jude the Obscure* by Dorset's native novelist Thomas Hardy. However there has been a hostelry on this site for over a thousand years and the cellars are thought to date back to these earliest times. It is here that the phantom monk lurks. In Saxon times there was no strict seclusion for nuns so monks were frequent visitors and often played an active role in the work of the abbey. Who this monk was and how he is linked to the cellars of the Grosvenor remain uncertain. He is seen infrequently and usually slips out of sight within seconds.

Rather more active is the Grosvenor's other ghost. This is a lady dressed in a long grey dress who moves purposefully around the upper floors. She is quite clearly in some distress and seems to be searching for something. What she has lost and why it is upsetting her so

The impressive Grosvenor Hotel, home to some odd paranormal activity.

much are as obscure as the antics of the monk in the cellar.

Turn left, with the Grosvenor on the right and turn right down the alley where the High Street turns left. This alley opens out into a broad promenade with a tall wall on the right and public gardens on the left. The gardens offer magnificent views south across the north Dorset countryside. The wall on the right hides the scanty ruins of the old Abbey, open in the summer only. Half way along the walk stands the town war memorial and a lane turns off to the right.

2) This is Abbey Walk.

It is along this pleasant walk that the troublesome ghost of the last monk of Shaftesbury might be encountered. Hearing that King Henry's men were on their way to shut the Abbey and confiscate its wealth, Abbess Elizabeth Souche decided to take action. At the time it was by no means certain that Henry's actions would be the end of the matter. The King had broken with the Pope and set up the Church of England for personal and political as much as religious reasons. Abbess Souche believed that the political climate might change and that she would again be allowed to continue her sacred calling. Things did not turn out that way and England was to become a Protestant nation.

But, hoping for the best, Abbess Souche collected together the gold, silver and other moveable wealth of the Abbey and entrusted it to a large, burly monk to hide in safety. The man set off, loaded down with his sack of valuables at dusk. He returned, covered in dirt and carrying a spade, soon after dawn. The treasure was, he declared, safe. King Henry's commissioners closed down the Abbey and confiscated its lands and buildings to the Crown. The nuns were given small pensions and sent on their way.

At this point Abbess Souche received an urgent message. The burly monk had been taken ill and wanted to speak to her. She hurried to his bedside. Desperately the man tried to tell her where he had hidden the treasure, but words failed him and he died without telling his secret.

Obviously the matter troubled his conscience. He returns to Abbey Walk from time to time, beckoning people to follow him into the gardens that now cover the steep slopes that once fell away from the Abbey walls. A few people have followed him in the hope of unearthing a treasure, but he always vanishes from sight before pointing out any spot in particular. Whatever is buried here seems certain to remain there for some time to come.

Return along the broad promenade. At the end bear right down the alley named Park Walk. This emerges at the rear of the Town Hall. A cobbled lane runs off to the right, plunging steeply down the side of the hill on which Shaftesbury is built. This is Gold Hill, one of the most famous streets in England. Its picturesque nature and quaint charm have ensured it has been featured in adverts, movies and television dramas and will be instantly recognisable to visitors.

The phantoms of Gold Hill date back over a thousand years. None of the houses that now line the street were then standing and the steep road formed the main entrance to the fortress town of Shaftesbury. It was up this hill that two men led a pack horse on a still evening in the year 978. On the horse was loaded the corpse of the recently murdered King Edward, soon to be known as the Martyr. Edward had been treacherously done to death at Corfe Castle, where his ghost re-enacts the killing, and his body was sent to Shaftesbury as the nearest holy house suitable for a royal burial. His killers did not, however, want to accord their victim much in the way of pomp and gave him just a pack horse as a hearse.

Edward's body was duly interred in the Abbey and before long miracles began to be reported. In 1001 Edward the Martyr was canonised. The cult of St Edward attracted many

The long walk beside the site of the ruined Abbey where a ghostly monk has been seen on numerous occasions.

pilgrims and brought wealth to the Abbey. It is the fateful arrival of the king's body that is re-enacted on Gold Hill. Two men dressed in tunics and cloaks lead a horse up the hill, over the pack is thrown the lifeless body of a young man - Edward was only 16 when killed - which lolls gruesomely as the horse paces up the slope.

3) Walk down Gold Hill and at the base turn left.Follow this lane along the base of the hill to a crossroads.

4) To take the optional excursion into the countryside, turn right down French Mill Lane. To return to the town centre, turn left up Great Lane.

A short distance along French Mill Lane there is a fork, take the left hand lane, which is the continuation of French Mill Lane. The first couple of hundred yards of French Mill Lane are lined by large houses set back behind fine gardens. After a while the lane becomes more rural, passing between fields. Where the lane plunges into a sunken section between high hedges the walk reaches the haunted section.

Back in medieval times this stretch of lane could be an exciting place to be of an evening. The holy nuns of Shaftesbury rigorously enforced the teachings of the Church within their town. For the soldiers of the garrison in the fortress, this was understandably irksome. So those in search of a bit of fun would make their way down French Mill Lane to the spot between high hedgerows where the Abbey's lands ended and those of a more broadminded lord of the manor began. Here they could dance, sing, drink and generally enjoy themselves.

One Sunday a group of soldiers was playing at cards, something firmly forbidden in the holy town of Shaftesbury, when a well-dressed stranger arrived. He asked what the men were

The market which takes place in Shaftesbury on most days and offers some tempting refreshments to walkers.

up to, playing and drinking in a lane, and was told of the ban on such activities in the town. The stranger declared he would stop for some entertainment before going into such a cheerless town, and sat down to play cards. The man played with skill and was soon winning a tidy sum, but then he dropped a card. One of the soldiers bent to pick it up and was horrified to see a hoof poking out from the stranger's trousers.

Leaping up with a cry of alarm, the soldier announced his discovery to his startled friends. The stranger threw off his disguise and declared that his game was only just beginning, inviting the soldiers to play for their souls against earthly wealth. None were keen on the offer, but took to their heels.

For generations afterwards this lane had an evil reputation. Bad things were said to happen here and the place was avoided after dark.

5) Just beyond this sunken section of lane is a T-junction. Turn right and follow the twisting, single track lane until it emerges at the fork in the road where the path turned left along French Mill Lane. Continue straight on to the crossroads, then cross over to climb up Great Lane.

6) At the top of Great Lane turn left along Salisbury Street to a five-way junction. Take the second left road into Shaftesbury High Street, lined by shops, ancient pubs and a fine church. A market is held here on certain weekdays. At the end of the High Street, turn right to reach the Grosvenor Hotel and to return to the car park.

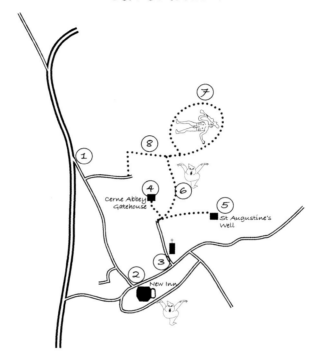

Walk No.3
Cerne Abbas

Cerne Abbey
Gatehouse

St Augustine's
Well

New Inn

The "Rude Man of Cerne", a gigantic chalk hill figure of indeterminate age, dominates the village and the valley in which it lies.

CerneAbbas

Distance:	**1.75 miles**
Ghostly Rating:	*** ***
Route:	**Cerne Abbas**
Map:	**OS Explorer 117**
Start/ Parking:	**Cerne Abbas**
Public Transport:	**Cerne Abbas is served by a frequent bus service running between Dorchester and Sherborne.**
Conditions:	**A short walk which runs around the village of Cerne Abbas to take in not only the local ghosts, but also a sacred spring and the famous Cerne Abbas Giant – a hill figure of famously rude appearance.**
Refreshments:	**Cerne Abbas has two tea shops and several pubs that offer reasonable fare to the visitor.**

Cerne Abbas is famous for its hill figure which dominates the surrounding countryside. It is of a naked, club-wielding giant with an erect penis. Inevitably the village has a variety of humorous souvenirs for sale which feature this rude figure in a number of guises. Giant apart, this is a charming village which was formerly the site of an ancient Benedictine Abbey and is still the site of extensive legends, folklore and, of course, ghosts.

The Walk

1) Park in the small car park above the village, off the A352, signed as Giant's View. This spot offers a fine view across the valley to the Giant.

The great chalk figure of the Cerne Abbas Giant is best known for his startling and very obvious nudity. His erect manhood measures an impressive 23 feet in length. The giant wields a huge club over 120 feet in length. Unlike most other hill figures, this giant has eyes, eyebrows, mouth, ribs and other features accurately rendered, he is no mere outline drawing. It has been estimated that to cut away the turf to reveal the chalk would have meant excavating around 25 tons of material, as well as having the know-how to render accurately such a gigantic figure on a hillside. Clearly this was a major undertaking for somebody, but who?

There is no written record of the giant before the 1690s when he is mentioned in the records of the local church, but this is no clear evidence for its age. Until Cerne began to be used as a stop by the coaches on the new roads of the 18th century this was a remote

The New Inn at Cerne which, despite its name, is one of the oldest buildings in the village.

area. Few gentlemen likely to record the giant would have come this way, and the locals would have known the giant far too well to comment on him. In 1754 a visiting doctor noted that the figure looked a bit like Hercules with his club, and that the lord of the manor provided food and drink every seven years for men to scour the figure and so keep it pristine.

Some suggested the giant was cut by the Club Raisers. This sturdy group of Dorset men organised themselves to drive off soldiers of either side in the Civil Wars of the 1640s. Their interest in politics or religion was slim compared to their determination to keep their crops for themselves. Lacking guns, these men carried clubs. This would certainly explain the giant's club, but would not explain his ruder aspect. Others suggest that the giant was cut by Denzil Holles, a Parliamentarian commander in the Civil War, who owned land in Cerne and was known for his satirical writings. If the giant is a 17th century satire, his significance is lost. Other suggested culprits include the Romans, the Phoenicians, the Celts, King Alfred and the monks who once owned Cerne and had a beautiful Abbey in the valley. In truth, nobody really knows how old this giant is nor for how many years he has been staring out across the valley of Cerne.

After viewing the hill figure, leave the car park down the lane to the right and walk down into the village of Cerne Abbas. In the centre of the village the lane ends in a T-junction.

2) Facing the lane exit is the New Inn.

This pub has the distinction of being haunted by two ghosts. As a large public building, the pub has been put to many uses over the years. In the 17th and 18th centuries the local courts were held here. The room that now serves as the front bar was a form of waiting room for those who would be appearing in court, be it as witness, lawyer or accused. One of these men still returns to haunt the room. He sits quietly in a phantom chair with his back to the wall. Then he looks up as if his name has been called. Getting to his feet he walks through the door into the passageway beyond that led to the court itself. Once in the passage he vanishes. The man appears often enough for details of his dress to be fairly certain. He wears riding boots over tight trousers and a long, dark coat with large, bright buttons. Most likely he dates back to around 1820, but who he is remains unclear.

The second ghost, or ghosts, appear in the garden at the rear of the pub. These happy phantoms are of two young children who run around playing with each other under the watchful and benevolent eye of an old

The ghostly gentleman of the New Inn.

The haunted bar of the New Inn, Cerne. The ghost who appears here is so natural in appearance that some witnesses do not realise they are seeing a phantom.

lady, perhaps their grandmother. These ghosts do not appear so often as the man in the bar. They may, however, appear at any time of year and it is the incongruous nature of young children playing outside in summer clothes in the depth of winter that tends to attract attention. It must be suspected that in the summer months they may pass for real children and not be noticed.

Leave the New Inn, turning right along the main street of the village.

3) Turn left in front of the Royal Oak and walk past the church on the right.

4) At the end of this lane, you can go straight ahead, if the gardens are open, to view the gatehouse of the ruined Cerne Abbey.

5) Having viewed the gatehouse, enter the graveyard through the gate. The path forks just beyond the gate. Take the right hand fork across the churchyard to reach the holy well of Cerne Abbas.

This well goes by the name of St Augustine's Well. According to legend, St Augustine came to this valley in the 590s to preach Christianity. As proof of the power of his God, the churchman struck the ground with his staff and created a spring of pure water at this spot. The folk of Cerne were not impressed, however, and drove the Christians out of their village. They came back, of course, and the spring was rediscovered by St Edwold from East Anglia in the 870s when he sought safety here from the marauding Vikings who had destroyed his home.

In more recent years, the spring gained a reputation for being able to heal weak eyesight and for being good for the health of pregnant women. It is also said that an unmarried girl can discover the identity of her future husband if she comes here at dawn on Midsummer's Day. She should come alone, kneel beside the spring and as the sun rises recite the ditty

> St Catherine, St Catherine
> O lend me thine aid
> And grant that I never
> May die an Old Maid
> A husband, St Catherine
> A good one, St Catherine
> But any one better than
> Not a one, St Catherine.

In these more politically correct days, of course, the old charm is not much used.

The well has recently been renovated and a new altar erected here.

6) Return to the fork in the path, turn right across the graveyard to a finely carved stone archway. Go through this gate into an open field. This is the site of the old Abbey.

The Abbey was founded in 987 and dominated the area for centuries. In 1987 the people of Cerne Abbas undertook a pilgrimage from Wells to mark the millennium of the founding

of the Abbey. The pilgrimage ended with a service in this field, the site of the long lost Abbey. They may have had watchers of which they were unaware for the ghosts of the holy monks of Cerne have been reported wandering quietly around this field. Seen most often at dawn, the monks are unobtrusive as they glide silently around long vanished corridors, cloisters and cells.

Continue across the open field, following the signs to Giant Hill.

7) The path emerges at the base of the slope on which the giant is carved. A path runs up the steep hill to circle the giant. At the top of the hill is the Trendle, a strange earthwork the date and purpose of which are as mysterious as those of the giant himself.

8) Continue around the hill figure, returning down the hill to the base of Giant Hill. A path runs to the right back to the Giant's View car park.

The gate to the churchyard at Cerne.

The sacred well at Cerne, around which many legends swirl and which may be as old as the mighty giant which overlooks it.

Gentle phantoms of centuries long gone by flit around this field just outside the village of Cerne Abbas.

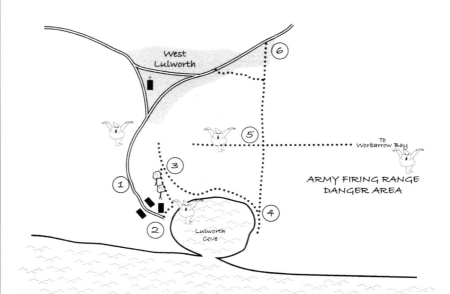

Walk No.4
Lulworth Cove

West
Lulworth

To
Worbarrow Bay

ARMY FIRING RANGE
DANGER AREA

Lulworth
Cove

The beach in Lulworth Cove where the enigmatic ghosts caused a security scare during the summer of 1940.

Lulworth Cove

Distance:	**2 miles or 7 miles**
Ghostly Rating:	*** * * ***
Route:	**Around Lulworth Cove**
Map:	**OS Explorer OL15**
Start/ Parking:	**Lulworth Cove Car Park**
Public Transport:	**Lulworth is served by a frequent bus service from both Poole and Dorchester.**
Conditions:	**A short but strenuous walk that involves something of a scramble, but is rewarded by spectacular views.**
Refreshments:	**Lulworth Cove is a magnet for tourists and day trippers. There are numerous places to eat or drink and something can be found to suit most tastes and pockets. The Beach Cafe welcomes walkers and provides good solid fare.**

Lulworth Cove does not go in for subtlety. At the exit from the car park is a large sign with bold letters advertising a shop with the words "Cream Teas". The access to the army's gun ranges is guarded by an equally frank sign reading "No entry. Risk of sudden death". The scenery is spectacular as well as charming, offering sweeping views as well as quaint cottages and the very epitome of a chocolate box cover version of an English village. The ghosts, on the other hand, are not quite what one might expect in so obviously English a place.

The Walk

1) Park in the main car park provided for visitors. The charges here are high, so it is as well that this is a short walk. Exit the car park through the walkway to the right of the Heritage Centre and bear right down a narrow lane towards the Cove. The end of the lane opens out on to the beach.

This beach is a quaint and attractive one now used only by a few local fishermen who have managed to, so far, evade the axe wielded by the European Union. In its time, however, it has been a small, but busy, port which imported all sorts of goods for the uses of local people. It has also had its share in the smuggling trade. What, if any, of these have given rise to the strange phantoms of the beach is unknown.

The ghosts first came to be known about during the Second World War. Along with all other beaches and coves which might offer a suitable landing place to German raiders or even invaders, Lulworth Cove was closed to the public. The beach was strewn with mines and barbed wire, while the road leading inland was blocked with anti-tank traps and other obstacles. It was, quite simply, impossible for anyone to get on or off the beach by land or sea. To make doubly certain that the area was proof against Hitler's invading hordes, lookouts were posted on the hills to sweep the seas and skies with binoculars.

It was with some amazement that the lookouts one night saw people down on the beach. They seemed to be dancing in the moonlight. Then they were gone. The area was carefully searched and the defences tested and repositioned. But the dancers came back a few weeks later. It subsequently emerged that the phantom dancers had been seen before. A yachtsman who anchored here in the 1930s

The wooded path that climbs from the beach to the cliffs above Lulworth Cove.

reported that the young people attracted his attention when they waded up out of the sea, and only later did they dance on the sands.

2) Just before the lane ends on the beach a flight of steps climbs up the hill to the left, behind the Beach Cafe. The steps are signposted to Bindon Hill. At the top of these steps the path runs off to the left, climbing steeply up the hill between trees and gorse. The path eventually reaches a stile on the far side of which a path runs left to right.

3) Turn right and keep close to the fence on your right hand side. Where a stile crosses the fence, go straight on along the path signed to the Fossil Forest, ignoring the path to the

left. As the path runs around the shoulder of the hill it offers magnificent views down to Lulworth Cove and along the coast.

4) When the path reaches a second stile the way forward is blocked by a barbed wire fence which marks the boundary of the army firing range. Turn left, signposted to Range Walks. At the summit of the hill is the entrance to the army ranges.

Lulworth Cove, seen from the ancient fortress that tops the cliffs high above.

The summit of this hill has its

ghosts. In around 400BC the easily defended hill was surrounded by earthen ditches and ramparts topped by wooden palisades. This was as a stronghold of the Durotiges, the Celtic tribe who inhabited this area. It was almost certainly occupied by those who made a living by sending out their fishing boats from Lulworth Cove and may have been a harbour for ships conducting trade with the

The haunted hilltop above Lulworth where a battle of long ago is recreated.

Celtic tribes of Gaul, as France was then known. But it is not these Celts whose ghosts roam this windswept summit.

In AD44 the Romans came to Dorset. Under their general Vespasian, who was later to become Emperor, the Legion II stormed into the lands of the Durotiges, capturing their previously invincible hillforts. Bindon Hill was one of those to fall to the Romans. Legend has it that one detachment of Romans was left to camp here after the battle, to ensure that the Celts did not return to reoccupy their old home. The wily Celts, however, waited for a foggy dawn, then crept up to the heights above Lulworth Cove. Pretending to launch an attack then to retreat, the tribesmen lured the Romans into a charge which led them directly over the cliffs where they fell to their deaths.

It is these luckless Romans who return night after night to haunt the heights of Bindon Hill. It is said that local people can predict when the legions will march, as the village dogs cower indoors and refuse to go out.

5) If the Ranges are open, and they usually are not, you can follow the path to Worbarrow Bay. Be very careful never to stray off the marked footpath. The army uses live ammunition here and unexploded artillery shells litter the ground. Only the paths are swept clear by the army. As the none-too-subtle sign warns on entering the area. There is a "Risk of Sudden Death".

In the late 17th century, Worbarrow Bay was a favourite landing place for smugglers. The bay offered sheltered waters and a gentle beach on which to land goods from France. At the same time it was remote enough to avoid prying eyes from villagers or fishermen honest enough to report what they saw to the revenue men.

One night a boatload of smugglers was landing brandy when a patrol of revenue men appeared. The smugglers' schooner set sail, leaving one of their comrades on the beach as the forces of law scrambled down the hill to the shore. The luckless smuggler tried to swim out to the safety of his boat, but became caught in the racing tide. While the revenue men threw stones and shot their guns, the man tried desperately to swim back to land, but in vain. His terrified screams tore the air as he struggled, then slipped beneath the waves.

That fateful night was in the waning quarter of the moon. To this day, on cloudless nights as the moon wanes, piercing screams echo around Worbarrow Bay. Some claim to be able

The charming village of West Lulworth which stands just inland of the cove that bears its name.

to see a man splashing desperately in the shallows, before slipping out of sight. Since the army took over the area there have been few, if any, people in Worbarrow Bay at night. As a result this particular ghost has not been seen for decades past.

Return to the entrance to the Range Walk. Turn right, keeping the range boundary fence on your right.

If the Ranges are closed, and they usually are, continue straight on past the entrance, keeping the range boundary fence on your right. The walk down the hill is a steep scramble. Where the path crosses the prehistoric earthwork, now reduced to a bank and ditch, the path bends to the left. Continue straight on along the narrower path between the gorse which is signed to the Youth Hostel. Cross over the stile from the scrubby hillside into an open grassy field. Walk across the field, close to the left hand side, to the gate at the far side of the field.

6) Go through the gate to the lane and turn left. Follow the lane through the picturesque village of West Lulworth. Keep left, ignoring any lanes to the right. Where the houses of the village peter out a farm is visible across the fields to the right.

This is Hambury Farm, and the road close to its entrance has an evil reputation. In the days when Lulworth was a busy little port, coaches frequently picked up passengers to take them inland to the towns and manors of Dorset. Aware that some passengers were persons of wealth, a highwayman decided to hold up the coach and chose this spot to commit his crime.

When the coach came into sight, the highwayman stepped forward in time-honoured fashion to declare "Stand and Deliver". But this was to be no ordinary crime for the coach driver put up a fight. In the ensuing struggle the driver was killed and fell beneath the wheels of his coach, which crushed his neck and severed his head. The highwayman escaped, but without any booty. It is the unfortunate driver whose ghost returns to haunt the site. Standing headless, he wanders about this stretch of road. Sometimes he is seen driving his coach, but such sightings seem to be rare.

Continue along this lane until the car park comes into view on the right.

The stretch of road inland from the cove where the highwayman lay in wait for his victims.

A highwayman holds up a coach. The ghost that lurks on the road outside West Lulworth commemorates a robbery such as this.

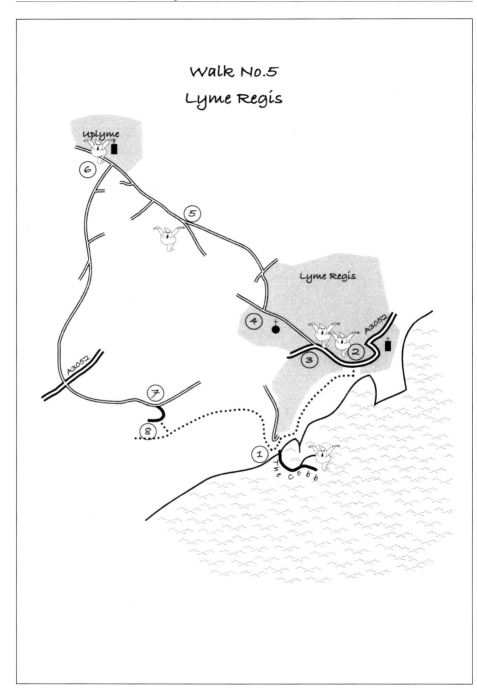

Walk No.5
Lyme Regis

Lyme Regis

Distance:	**4 miles**
Ghostly Rating:	✱ ✱ ✱ ✱ ✱
Route:	**Lyme Regis - Uplyme - Lyme Regis**
Map:	**OS Explorer 116**
Start/ Parking:	**The Cobb car park**
Public Transport:	**Lyme Regis is served by an hourly bus service from Bridport and less frequent services to other towns.**
Conditions:	**A fairly long walk which has one or two steep hills included. This route takes in the town centre of Lyme Regis, including the famous Cobb harbour and waterfront, as well as some quiet inland country areas.**
Refreshments:	**As a commercial town and favourite of visiting tourists, Lyme Regis has many pubs, cafes and snack bars.**

The spectacular centrepiece of the walk is the Cobb, Lyme Regis's famous harbour waterfront which has featured in movies and television dramas. Lyme itself is a charming little town with much to offer the visitor. It also has its fair share of ghosts, most of them linked to the tragic Monmouth Rebellion which took place over three centuries ago, but which still has dark memories in the West Country.

The Walk

1) Park in the Cobb car park, signposted from all routes into Lyme. From the car park walk on to the Cobb to view the harbour.

The supernatural came to the Cobb in truly spectacular fashion in the late 17th century. As evening drew in one moonless evening a ship of foreign appearance put in here. The sails were black and the men who worked the rigging neither spoke nor seemed to have any interest in

Lyme's harbour, the Cobb, has been visited by several movie companies, but once played host to a far more terrible visitor.

Lyme's Royal Lion pub which has been the centre of persistent rumours of otherworldly activity.

their surroundings. They moved as if bereft of all hope. The ship tied up to the Cobb and the captain came ashore. He spoke to no one and looked neither to left nor to right. Dressed in black clothes of fine quality and fashionable cut the mysterious captain strode along the Cobb and into Lyme.

Marching up Silver Street, the foreigner came to the house of Mayor Jones. Mayor Jones was one of the richest men in Dorset, but not one of the most popular. He was a religious zealot of fervour who used his wealth and position to persecute those who disagreed with him. He scorned any who questioned his views, was contemptuous of Catholics, but had a special hatred for non-conformists.

The stranger eyed the house for a moment, then kicked the door in. The entire wall of the house collapsed into the street with a thundering crash. "I've come for you, Jones," shouted the stranger as he walked amid the debris. As terrified witnesses stared, the man grabbed Jones by the shoulder and dragged him down to the Cobb. Jones seemed powerless to resist as the silent crew cast off and hoisted the sails. As silently and mysteriously as the ship had come, it glided out to sea.

Bizarrely, the body of Mayor Jones was found among the tumbled wreckage of his house, although dozens had seen him dragged on board the strange ship. It was widely believed that the Devil himself had come to Lyme in his dreaded Black Ship of Death to claim the soul of Old Jones.

2) Walk along the seafront to the foot of Silver Street where a cannon looks out to sea. Walk up Silver Street until you reach the Royal Lion on the right side of the road.

This pub has long had a reputation for being haunted, though by what is not quite so clear. The upstairs rooms are often visited by a vague grey shape which slides silently along the corridor. The thing is about the size and height of a human, but no features are readily apparent. On separate occasions the sound of somebody in heavy boots has been heard walking down the same corridor. Whether or not the two phenomena are related is a mystery.

Continue up the hill to find Boots on the right. Now a shop, this was formerly a large private house which went by the name of Chatham House.

The notorious "Bloody" Judge Jeffreys whose phantom lurks in Lyme Regis more than three centuries after his fatal visit.

It was in this house that the dreaded Judge George Jeffreys stayed when he came to Lyme in September 1685 to try those local men who had joined the rebellion of the Duke of Monmouth. Monmouth was the illegitimate son of King Charles II who had died earlier that year.

The Protestant Monmouth landed from exile in Lyme Regis in June 1685 and raised a rebellion against the new king, his Catholic uncle James II. The uprising was in the name of the Protestant religion and against the failings of the new king's petulant and incompetent rule. The West Country rose to support Monmouth, but the rest of the country was unconvinced and stayed at home. In the face of the royal army, the western farm boys had little hope and they lost the only battle of the campaign at Sedgemoor in Somerset. Monmouth was executed in London, but James II decreed that his followers had to be tried and executed in their home towns.

Chatham House is one of the more haunted sites in Lyme Regis.

And so Judge Jeffreys came to Lyme Regis to try the 12 local men who had joined Monmouth. A verdict of not guilty was not an option in the biased court run by Jeffreys. Elsewhere the judge had handed down sentences of execution on the wretches dragged before him, though these had often been commuted to flogging or transportation if a suitable bribe was offered. But Jeffreys was determined to make an example of Lyme, the first town visited by Monmouth. All were to hang, though Jeffreys had not told anyone of his decision.

The trial of the 12 men took place on 11 September. All were found guilty and all were duly sentenced to death. That night Jeffreys and his lawyers retired to Chatham House where they spent £25 of Lyme money on a banquet which included 15 gallons of wine. The sum is preserved in the town accounts.

According to local legend it was towards the end of this boozy evening that a young lady came to Chatham House to beg for the life of her brother, one of those found guilty that day. Knowing the judge's liking for bribes, the girl brought a bag of coins. Jeffreys promised to change the sentence to a flogging, but only if the lady would spend the night with him. The distraught girl did as instructed and sacrificed her honour for her brother's life. Next morning, she climbed out of the Judge's bed and dressed herself. When she left Chatham House it was to find her brother's body swinging with the others from the gallows erected on the beach.

Perhaps deservingly, Judge Jeffreys has not rested easy. He returns to Chatham House in spectral form wearing his judge's robes and wearing the black cap worn when administering

The Black Dog inn, formerly a pub, is named after the local spectre.

the death penalty. He carries in his hand a bloodstained bone, though the significance of this is unclear. The judge appears most often at night, walking slowly from room to room with an odd shuffling gait.

3) Continue up the hill. Where the main road bends left, signposted A3052 to Seaton, continue straight on along Silver Street. Pass the church on the left.

4) Where a large stone house stands on the right, turn right into Haye Lane. Follow this narrow lane to a staggered junction, where the walk goes straight on.

5) This lane emerges on to a wider road beside the Black Dog Hotel, formerly a pub but now a bed and breakfast.

The building took its name from the local spectral creature. This stretch of road is haunted by one of England's most widespread and dangerous ghosts, that of Black Shuck. This phantom takes the form of a gigantic hound covered with long, shaggy black hair. Its eyes are said to be perfectly round and to glow with an eerie inner fire as if they are hot coals. This startling apparition is said to be an evil spirit able to bring bad luck and even death to those that see it. Anyone foolish enough to approach the dog as it runs along roads and paths across England can expect nothing but ill fortune. The only reasonably safe course is to get out of the way and stay there. Running away is to be recommended.

Such is the great phantom hound which patrols this stretch of what is now the B3165. The ghost itself might be enough to give the pub its name, but the two have a more intimate connection. Late one night in the 18th century the Black Dog was seen trotting along the road from Lyme. When it reached this inn, it gave the building a venomous glare and struck it with its tail. Next day the corner of the building collapsed. After the rebuilding the pub was renamed after the hell hound that had left its mark.

6) Turn right along the road, pausing beside the third lane on the left.

This stretch of road runs inland, skirting the little village of Uplyme. It was along this road that the Duke of Monmouth rode inland in June 1685 at the beginning of his fatal rebellion. The Duke was tall, handsome and extremely popular. Nell Gwynne, his father's mistress, had once said that Monmouth should inherit the throne "because kings should be handsome". Many others would have preferred to see Monmouth on the throne in place of his uncle, but not strongly

The Coast Path runs through scrub above Lyme Regis.

enough to come out and bear arms for him. Monmouth's reception at Lyme, Uplyme and other places as he progressed inland was warm and tumultuous, but he lacked the military might to enforce his claim.

It is this happy time that Monmouth's ghost recreates here at Uplyme. Mounted on a black stallion of noble bearing, the ghost of this handsome young man rides along waving his plumed hat at an invisible crowd of cheering locals. The ghost is rarely visible for long at any one time. The phantom's appearances are as fleeting as was poor Monmouth's earthly happiness.

Turn left up this lane. Continue along the narrow lane as it runs up a hill and through open countryside to the A3052. Cross the A3052 into another single track lane.

7) Follow this lane down hill to a narrow drive on the right signposted "The Crow's Nest" and signed as a public footpath. This drive curves to the right.

8) At a sign post indicating the Coast Path, turn left. This meets the South West Coast Path almost immediately. Turn left. Go through the gate with the National Trust sign and continue along this path until it meets a metal gate on the left. Bear right, pass a wooden fence and bear right again to climb over a stile. Follow this path as it drops steeply down a hill through woodland. In places the path forms a flight of steps. This path emerges through a caravan park into the Cobb car park.

The narrow flight of steps that leads down from the Coast Path to the Cobb.

Walk No.6
Corfe Castle and Knowle Hill

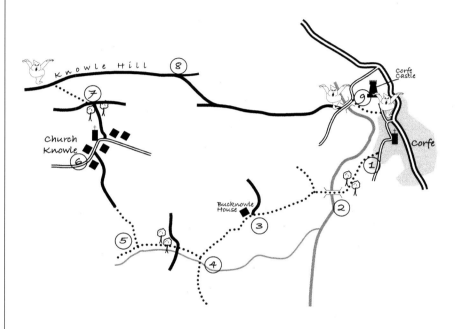

Corfe Castle, as seen from the car park at the start of the walk.

Corfe Castle and Knowle Hill

Distance:	**4.75 miles**
Ghostly Rating:	*** * ***
Route:	**Corfe Castle - Church Knowle - Knowle Hill - Corfe Castle**
Map:	**OS Explorer OL15**
Start/ Parking:	**Corfe Castle Car Park, off High Street**
Public Transport:	**Corfe is served by a railway station and by an hourly bus service running between Swanage and Wareham.**
Conditions:	**A fairly strenuous walk with a steep climb up to Knowle Hill and down again. The path in the valley floor, alongside the stream, can be wet after rain. There are several stiles to negotiate and they may be slippery when wet.**
Refreshments:	**There are plenty of pubs, tea rooms and such in Corfe Castle.**

The Isle of Purbeck has more ghosts than the local people know what to do with. Some of the oldest and most dramatic are to be encountered on this walk. The village of Corfe Castle is, of course, named after the magnificent ruin that dominates this area and guards the gap in the hills which leads into the Isle of Purbeck. This has been a strategic spot for generations of military commanders, so it is no surprise that the ghosts here have a distinctly martial air. Today the village is largely given over to catering to the needs of the tourists who visit the castle, so there is no shortage of places to eat, relax and recuperate after this strenuous walk.

The Walk

1) Park in the Council Car Park, signposted from the village centre – or walk there if arriving by public transport. Leave by the kissing gate near the pay machine beside the exit.

From this field you can look to your right to take in magnificent views of the towering castle ruins. The long, steep hill to the left of the castle is Knowle Hill along which the walk later passes.

Walk straight across the field in front of you to a second kissing gate, this one with stone walls. Pass through a patch of woodland and then cross a grassy area to cross over a stream by way of a small stone bridge (2).

Pass through the gate beyond. Ignore the path to your right, but strike straight across the field to exit via a gap in the hedge to the left of the clump of trees visible on the far side of the field. A broad track runs up the right hand side of this field to a farm, Bucknowle House.

3) Just before the farm the track turns right, you need to cross the stile straight in front of you to enter a field. Keep to the right side of the field as you skirt the farm grounds. When you reach the far side of this field, pass through a gap in the fence. Strike out diagonally left across this field towards the left side of a clump of trees. The field slopes down steeply here and the grass can be slippery when wet.

4) At the base of the slope ignore the path to your left which crosses the stream, but walk along the right bank of the stream. Climb over a stile to cross over a gravel track. Stay beside the stream to enter a path through a patch of woodland. A stile takes the path from the woodland into a field, stay beside the stream as you walk across this field, climb over another stile and cross another field. At the far side of this field a stile takes the path on to a wooden bridge.

5) Ignore this path and instead turn right to climb a steep and sometimes slippery hill. Over the crest of this rise the far side of the field comes into sight with a gate in the far left hand corner. This gate leads to a gravel track. Follow this track past various houses to the main street of the village of Church Knowle.

This village is one of the oldest on the Isle of Purbeck. For many years in the Saxon period this was the only place of Christian worship in the area, and it is this which gave the village its name. The church in question was replaced in 1225 by a new church, which still stands though it has been much altered.

6) At the main street, turn right and walk along this road for 100 yards to reach the Church of St Peter.

The church stands on the site of the earlier Saxon church, itself probably a replacement for a stone cross from which passing priests would preach the word of God to the local pagan farmers. As late as the time of the Domesday Book in 1087, Church Knowle was the only village in the Isle of Purbeck which had a permanent priest living in the village where he preached. It is worth paying a visit to the church as you pass. There is a small, but fine monument to the Clavell Family. Erected in 1572, this monument serves as a tomb for several members of this local family of gentry. The family came over with William the Conqueror in 1066 and was granted estates in this area by a grateful conqueror. Descendants of the family, through the female line, still own extensive acres around this village and inhabit the local manor.

Just beyond the church turn left and walk up the track which skirts on the right side of the churchyard. Pass through the gate and follow the green track which runs straight up the hill.

7) Where this path enters some woodland, cross a stile beside a gate. A signpost points left along a broad track to Cocknowle and right to Corfe Castle. Turn left, then almost immediately take a fork to the right. This path runs at an angle up Knowle Hill picking its way through the gorse and bracken until it meets a broad track running from left to right along the summit of the ridge.

To the left along this broad track is a small monument. This is a memorial to Mary Baxter MBE who was a great friend to the Dorset countryside and to the cause of keeping footpaths open in particular. The stone monument was erected by the Ramblers' Association and offers sweeping views to both north and south.

At the track turn right. This grassy track is broad, level and straight.

This is the old Roman road from Dorchester to Swanage Bay. The road is haunted by not one ghost, not two but by hundreds of them. An entire phantom army has been seen marching along this road, usually from east to west. The men step out in perfect unison, but in absolute silence. They look neither to right nor to left and studiously ignore anyone else on the path. With glittering helmets and shields slung over their shoulders, these men march purposefully forward. Those who have seen these men are in no doubt that they are Romans. They carry large oblong shields and have round helmets with cheek pieces. They are generally seen from below the hill. One moment they are absent, the next they are in sight, hundreds of them marching in column. The viewers watch as the column of marching men pass away until they vanish from sight into a fold in the hills, from which they never emerge.

8) After passing through gates and along the ridge, the old Roman road meets a fork. The old road goes straight on, but this is not a public right of way. Take the right hand fork. This path drops steeply down from the hill and meets a path running along the foot of the hill from the right. Bear left and follow this track along the foot of the hill until Corfe Castle comes back into sight. Where the path meets a road, turn left and cross a narrow stone bridge.

This bridge is haunted by a somewhat enigmatic lady in a flowing white dress. Local gossip has it that this is the phantom of Lady Banks who heroically held Corfe Castle for the cause of King Charles during the Civil Wars of the 17th century. By holding this fortress the small royalist garrison effectively stopped the Roundheads from using Swanage. By threatening to launch raids and surprise attacks, Lady Banks also closed Poole. The castle was too strategic for Oliver Cromwell to allow the noble Lady Banks to hold out forever. Eventually, powerful cannon were brought up to pound the defences. The mighty stone walls of Corfe were powerless against the state-of-the-art artillery of the 17th century. The Royalists were forced to surrender and Corfe Castle was 'slighted', meaning its defences were blown apart by gunpowder. Thereafter the castle was left to rot, and poor Lady Banks returned to haunt this little bridge.

9) On the other side of the bridge, turn right along a footpath signposted to the village centre. This path runs along the base of the steep hill on which the castle stands and emerges in the village market square.

This market square is haunted by the sound of pounding hoofbeats as a horse gallops by at breakneck speed. A clue as to who this ghost might be can be found in the sign that dominates the market place. This commemorates the murder and martyrdom of a King of England who was created a saint after his death. This unfortunate monarch was King Edward who came to the throne in 975.

The teenage Edward was a dashing, handsome young man who loved to indulge in the drinking, fighting and womanising expected of a nobleman of his time. Unlike most men of

The memorial to King Edward, murdered at Corfe by his own stepmother.

his type he was also a generous benefactor of the Church, endowing monasteries and cathedrals with estates of impressive size and wealth. But Edward's most outstanding characteristic was a tactlessness of truly heroic proportions. Within just three years of coming to the throne Edward had managed to upset just about everyone. Only the Archbishop of Canterbury, the recipient of so much wealth, had a good word to write about him. Edward himself was blithely unaware anything was wrong. It seems his arrogance was second only to his tactlessness.

Among the people he upset was his stepmother, Aelfryth. This was dangerous. Not only was she a proverbially unforgiving woman, but she had a son who was heir to the throne so long as Edward died without leaving a son.

One summer, Lady Aelfryth was staying at Corfe Castle with her young son. King Edward was hunting nearby and on a whim decided to visit his stepmother and half brother. The visit seemed to be cordial and a fine dinner was had by all. As the king was mounting his horse in the castle courtyard, his stepmother's trusted servant came forward with a last goblet of wine. Never one to refuse a drink, the king leant forward to take it – and was stabbed in the chest. Putting his spurs to his charger, the king bolted out of the castle at full gallop. His stepmother sent her retainers after him, but she need not have worried. The king was mortally wounded and toppled from his horse in the market square. He was dead when he hit the cobbles.

Is it the ghost of this murdered king who gallops through the Market Square of Corfe with such frantic haste? It is likely for no other man is known to have died here in such a way.

The small stone bridge that carries the walk over a stream.

As for Aelfryth and her son, they did not prosper by their crime. The son did indeed become king, but nobody ever trusted him again. When he needed an army, men failed to follow him. When he needed money, men delayed and avoided paying. This unfortunate king has gone down in history as Ethelred the Unready. And most unready he always was because of the murder done here in Corfe.

The eponymous church of Church Knowle is one of the oldest buildings in southern Dorset.

As you enter the Market Place, the entrance to the castle, owned by the National Trust, is to the left. Turn right to enter the High Street and return to the car park.

The old Roman road runs across the crest of Knowle Hill.

A Roman legion in battle order and carrying its standards to the fore. It is just such a legion that marches over Knowle Hill from time to time.

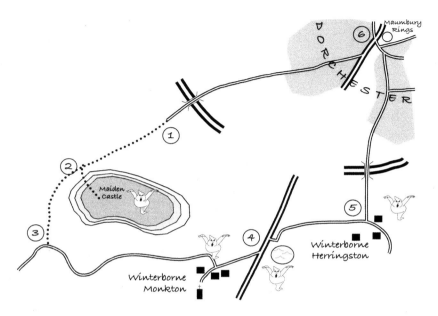

Walk No.7
Maiden Castle

The slopes of Maiden Castle rise up above the surrounding fields. The hill was once home to tens of thousands of local Celtic tribesmen.

Maiden Castle

Distance:	**5.5 miles**
Ghostly Rating:	★ ★ ★ ★
Route:	**Maiden Castle - Winterborne Monkton - Winterborne Herringston - Maumbury Rings - Maiden Castle**
Map:	**OS Explorer OL15**
Start/ Parking:	**Maiden Castle car park**
Public Transport:	**No public transport runs to Maiden Castle, but the walk can be accessed on foot from central Dorchester which has plentiful bus routes and two railway stations.**
Conditions:	**A bracing walk over the windy hills south of Dorchester. For most of the route the walk passes over surfaced lanes and tracks, but in places crosses open grassland which can be muddy when wet.**
Refreshments:	**There are no facilities for refreshments on this walk.**

Even on the finest days the wind can be surprisingly strong on these hills. On days when a breeze blows in the valleys, a positive gale can be felt on the course of this walk. The open countryside is host to some of the older ghosts of Dorset and to some of the most modern of bizarre phenomenon. It is possible to link this walk to the Dorchester town centre walk, which might be welcome as it is here that the walker will find pubs, cafes and restaurants to offer refreshment after this breezy jaunt.

The Walk

1) Park in the English Heritage car park at the southern end of Maiden Castle Road. Walk out of the southern end of the car park and follow the path up to Maiden Castle. Enter Maiden Castle, using the informative display boards to find your way to the scanty ruins of a late Roman temple.

The ghosts here are closely linked to the varied history of this mighty fortress. The site was first inhabited in the Neolithic period, around 4,500 years ago, when a small fortified farmstead stood here. This was later enlarged in around 600BC to form a fort surrounded by a single deep ditch at the eastern end of the hill. By 200BC the current massive fortress was in place. Covering 47 acres and surrounded by a triple ring of mighty ditches and

The steep ramparts of Maiden Castle which were once topped by wooden walls lined by ranks of Celtic warriors.

ramparts, this fortress was made even stronger than it appears today by timber and turf palisades crowning the ramparts. In 100BC the gates were remodelled to form the complex maze of paths and ditches that now protect the site.

None of these mighty works was enough to protect Maiden Castle when the Romans arrived in the shape of the General, and soon to be Emperor, Vespasian and the Legion II. In AD43 the local Celtic tribe, the Durotiges, defied the might of Rome from this fortress. The Romans attacked with powerful catapults able to hurl iron-tipped bolts as thick as a man's arm. The wooden palisades crumbled and the bravery of the Celts was not enough to hold back the disciplined legions.

Thereafter the Romans put a small garrison on the hilltop to dissuade any attempt at reoccupation and moved the Durotiges into a new town down in the valley of the River Frome. The new site was named Durnovaria and came to be the economic and governmental centre for much of what is now southwestern England. It is now known as Dorchester.

The ghosts of Maiden Castle appear to date from this period of its history. Clearly the locals had neither entirely forgotten nor abandoned their ancestral home on the windswept hill top. A small temple was erected here. Although built in Roman style and fashion it seems to have been dedicated to a local god. And it is here that the ghosts congregate. Dressed in the togas and tunics of civilian Romans, the phantoms stand and walk as if deep in conversation and oblivious to what goes on around them. It is likely that some sightings have not been reported as the phantoms might be mistaken for real people in fancy dress, or preparing for a film shoot. The glory of this pagan temple was not to last. When Christianity came to Dorset in the failing days of the Roman Empire the little temple was abandoned to the elements and Maiden Castle was finally deserted after almost 3,000 years.

2) Leave Maiden Castle but instead of returning to the car park walk straight ahead to pass through a gate and turn left along a track signposted simply as Bridlepath. Follow this track down the hill until it meets a lane.

3) At the lane, turn left and follow it into the little cluster of houses that make up Winterborne Monkton.

This charming village sits on the slopes that run down from the hill topped by Maiden Castle into the valley of the Winterborne stream. This narrow valley is said to be the haunt of a pair of Roman soldiers. Perhaps these are casualties of the attack on Maiden Castle, or they

A fight between Romans and Celts. Archaeological excavation has shown that a fight such as this raged around the slopes of Maiden Castle during the Roman invasion of the first century AD.

may be members of the subsequent garrison. Whoever they may be, these two men march with military step along the damp grassy meadows at the sides of the stream.

4) Continue along the lane to the A354. Cross the main road to find a wide pool of deep water.

This main road has been the chief link between Dorchester and Weymouth for 2,000 years. It runs along the exact same route as the Roman road built by Vespasian's legions, as can be deduced by its straight route. Some time in the past, nobody is entirely certain when, a coach was racing north from Weymouth towards Dorchester. As it came down the steep slope of Monkton Hill the coach gathered so great a speed that it got out of control. Terrified, but unable to stop, the horses plunged into this deep pool of water, dragging the coach in with them. The good folk of Winterborne Monkton hurried to help, but all they saw was a rapidly shrinking trail of bubbles and waves. There were no survivors. Time and again, this horrific accident has been played out in spectral form, though nobody would seem to have witnessed it in recent years.

Now walk a short distance north along the main road, before turning right along the lane that runs east. Follow this lane under the railway and into Winterborne Herringston.

It was here that one of the earliest manifestations of a very modern and bizarre mystery appeared in England. Where the road into the village takes a sharp turn right, the Winterborne stream is joined by another coming down from the northern slopes of Maiden Castle. A broad area of level ground lies around the confluence of the streams, beyond which is the steep ridge of Conygar Hill.

It was in the field at the base of this hill that Dorset's first crop circle formed in the early 1990s. The great circle of flattened corn measured over 125 feet in diameter. The circle appeared overnight, with no trace of any rational way in which it could have come into existence. Unlike some later circles, which many suspect to be the work of human tricksters, this was a simple circle. It is possible that the strong winds of these hills were whipped into some ferocious eddy by the peculiar shape of the meeting valleys. Such a circling gust of wind might have been enough to flatten the crops.

Of course, there are plenty of extraterrestrial and supernatural explanations for the phenomenon of crop circles. But whatever the truth behind them, this is where it all started.

5) Just before the village turn left. Follow this lane north, over the A35 and into the housing estates of suburban Dorchester. Ignore turnings to the right and follow this road until it reaches Maumbury Rings.

The impressive earthworks of Maumbury Rings date back to around 2000BC. There was no doubt some form of ceremonial purpose to these works for they are not suitable for defensive or agricultural uses. In Roman times the works were remodelled to form an amphitheatre for plays, gladiatorial combat and wild animal hunts. As late as the 17th century the rings were being used for bull-baiting and similar bloody sports. Dorchester was clearly a ceremonial centre of great importance in the misty dawn of prehistory. When a new supermarket was being built in the town centre the builders uncovered the remains of an even larger circular bank and ditch complex. This was similar to Maumbury Rings, but had been embellished with dozens of tree trunks set upright in the ground in a pattern similar to that of Stonehenge.

6) At Maumbury Rings, there is a choice. To link this walk with that in Dorchester town centre, turn right along the B3147 and follow the road until it reaches a crossroads with traffic lights. The turning on the right is High West Street, where the town centre walk can be picked up at point 6. Alternatively, the Maiden Castle walk can be completed. Turn left along the B3147 for a short distance, then turn right down the road signposted to Maiden Castle. Follow this road back to the car park.

A fatal accident to a Victorian coach led to a dramatic haunting on the main road from Dorchester to Weymouth.

Maumbury Rings construction.

Walk No.8
Cull-pepper's Dish

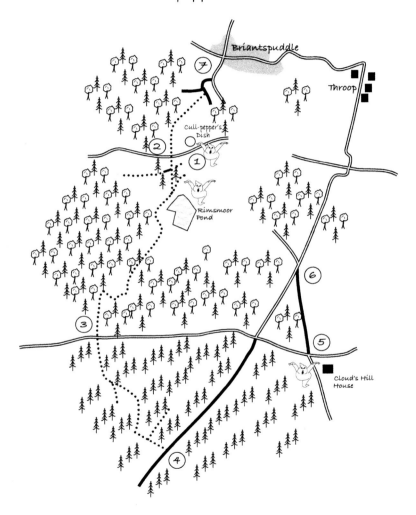

Briantspuddle

Throop

7

Cull-pepper's Dish

2

1

Rimsmoor Pond

6

3

5

Cloud's Hill House

4

Cull-pepper's Dish

Distance:	**6 miles**
Ghostly Rating:	* * *
Route:	**Cull-pepper's Dish - Cloud's Hill - Throop - Briantspuddle - Cull-pepper's Dish**
Map:	**OS Explorer 117**
Start/ Parking:	**Forestry Commission's Cull-pepper's Dish car park**
Public Transport:	**This walk can be accessed at Briantspuddle which is served by an infrequent bus service from Poole.**
Conditions:	**A delightful forest walk enlivened at times by the fact that the walk skirts an extensive army training ground used for cross-country tank and armoured vehicles manoeuvres. There are no steep hills and the surfaces are generally good, though they may be muddy in places.**
Refreshments:	**There are no facilities for refreshments on this walk.**

This walk takes in varied woodland scenery from mature oak forest to sterile commercial pine plantations. There are impressive views and enclosed forests. Much of the undergrowth in the southern part of the walk is composed of rhododendrons and, at the appropriate time of year, these make a truly spectacular display of blooms. Of the three phantoms that may be encountered here, by far the most famous is Lawrence of Arabia whose house at Cloud's Hill is owned by the National Trust and is open to the public during the summer months.

The Walk

1) Park in the small car park owned by the Forestry Commission which is located on the lane which turns east off the B3390 just south of Affpuddle and runs to Bere Regis. As you exit the car park on to the lane, Cull-pepper's Dish is behind the hedges directly in front of you. This impressive hollow is exceptionally steep and very deep. It is possible to climb down into it, but this is a scramble and the ground is very slippery when wet. Great care should be taken. Having viewed the dish, return to the road and turn right.

This stretch of road is haunted by a small group of ghosts which can be both seen and heard. Tramping steadily along the lane in perfect step with each other come four men

The road beside Cull-pepper's Dish where an ominous haunting has been reported.

carrying a coffin on their shoulders. There are no other mourners accompanying this cortege. It can only be assumed that this is the recreation of some funeral from long ago which ended at the little church in Turners Puddle, for there is no other cemetery within easy reach in the direction the men are walking.

2) About 50 yards from the Dish this lane is crossed by a footpath. This is part of the Ramblers' Association's Jubilee Trail. Turn left along the path signposted to Moreton. Follow the path downhill and across a patch of open heathland. Cross the first track the path meets, but turn right along the second track. A few yards along this track, look down the slope to the left to see the sinister waters of Rimsmoor Pond.

The stories that swirl around this bleak place are many. The pool is said to be bottomless and its waters are strangely deadly for no fish or other water creatures are to be found in its dark, silent expanse. There is said to be a malevolent spirit lurking here that lures passers-by to their deaths. It was one such death some years ago that led to the haunting of this dismal place.

The path runs through wooded hills south of Cull-pepper's Dish.

A young man from Briantspuddle was returning home after a convivial evening out with friends and foolishly chose to ride back by way of Bryants Heath, and to skirt the waters of Rimsmoor Pond. What happened exactly will never be known. The young man never came home, nor did his horse. Next morning his friends set out to trace his steps. When they reached the high ground above the pond, they saw the ground had been torn up by frantic hooves and the bushes torn aside as if some dreadful fight had taken place. Ominous skid marks showed where the horse had slid down the steep slope, straight into the waters of Rimsmoor Pond. Of the man and his horse there was no sign, just the empty wind blowing across the dark waters.

To this day the fading light of evening will sometimes show the doomed young man riding along the path towards Rimsmoor Pond. As he reaches the top of the rise, the ghostly man glances down towards the pond with a look of horror. Then he vanishes. Whatever happened to him was frightful. Best to avoid this spot after sunset.

Continue along the path. It is important to stay on the path as the surrounding land is marshy and boggy, even in the driest weather. It is easy to get stuck in a morass. Follow the path into woodland and stick to the path, ignoring side turnings, until it reaches a surfaced lane.

3) Cross the lane and go through a gate to join a narrow footpath through a copse of trees which emerges alongside an open field. Follow the path to the end of the field where it bends left to re-enter the woodland. Soon after the path passes a broken concrete pillar the Jubilee Trail turns right. Continue

The bleak, bottomless morass of Rimsmoor Pond which is surrounded by treacherous marsh and bog. This place has an evil reputation and a sad spectre.

straight on along the track which bends right, then left. Where a broad track turns left in a clearing, go straight on.

The doomed horseman whose ghost returns to Rimsmoor Pond to relive a terrifying horror.

4) Keep to the path until it passes between a pair of wooden posts and emerges on to a wide gravel track. Turn left and follow this wide track through the commercial forest plantations to a road. Turn right along the road to a lane from the right.

5) Turn right. On your left is Cloud's Hill house, the former home of Lawrence of Arabia and now owned by the National Trust.

This stretch of road is haunted around dawn by the throaty roar of a motorbike engine racing at full throttle. No motorbike ever comes into sight for this is a ghostly bike, a Brough Superior. It was on this bike that Lawrence of Arabia was killed in 1935. Lawrence had led an extraordinary life. He is best remembered for his exploits leading the Arab armies in World War I against the Turkish Empire. Combining the traditional mobile nature of the desert Arabs with his own knowledge of the wider war, Lawrence was able to achieve stunning victories against the odds. That the subsequent peace treaties failed to give the Arabs the independence they wanted was a bitter disappointment to Lawrence.

By the time the war broke out, however, Lawrence had already led an adventurous life. Born in Wales, he was educated at Oxford where he made the most of his gift for languages. He went to the valley of the Tigris and

The path south of Rimsmoor Pond passes through dense woodland before entering a commercial plantation.

The road outside Cloud's Hill House is haunted by the ghost of the house's most famous inhabitant.

Euphrates in 1911 to work as an archaeologist. There he helped Sir Flinders Petrie uncover much about the nature of ancient Assyria and the Babylonian Empire. After a spell in military intelligence in North Africa, Lawrence joined the Arabs and spent the next three years in the desert. Lawrence remained in the military after the war, but never seemed comfortable with his fame. He served under an assumed name and retired in 1935 to his home at Cloud's Hill. Within months he was dead.

It is not only his phantom bike that returns to this place. Lawrence himself has been seen in and around his old home. The white-washed walls of the cottage play host to his phantom as it walks quietly around. Sometimes he is dressed in the Arab robes which won him such fame, but on other occasions the ghost appears in comfortable country tweeds of the 1920s. It is to be hoped that his phantom can find the rest that was so often denied his restless spirit in life.

Retrace your steps along the side turning. Straight ahead is a bridleway striking into the woodland. Follow this bridleway until it emerges on to a narrow lane.

6) Turn right. Keep straight on along this lane until it enters the hamlet of Throop. All the land to the right of this lane belongs to the army and is used for tank exercises, which can be loud and spectacular. In Throop the lane bends left and runs across country to reach the village of Briantspuddle.

7) In the centre of the village the lane meets a junction. Turn left. About 100 yards along this road veer right up a track signposted to Cull-pepper's Dish. At a junction with a second track, turn left then almost immediately peel off right along a footpath marked by a Dorset County Council blue arrow. Where the path enters an open glade, turn left along a path signposted to Cull-pepper's Dish. This is where the walk rejoins the Jubilee Trail. Follow the trail through the woods to reach a surfaced lane. Turn left to return to the car park.

Mounted Arabs of Lawrence's forces cross a desert wadi during the last months of World War I.

The houses of Throop.

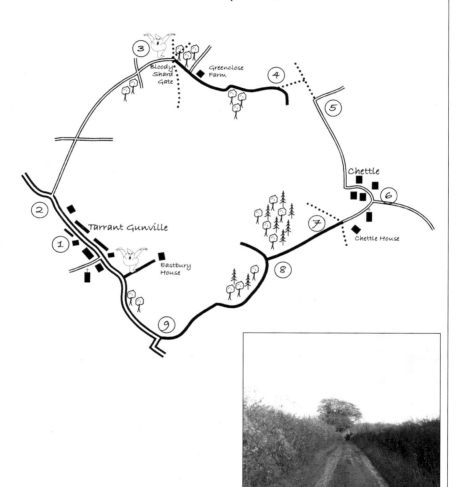

Walk No.9
Tarrant Gunville

3 Bloody Shard Gate
Greenclose Farm
4
5
Chettle
6
7
Chettle House
2
1 Tarrant Gunville
Eastbury House
8
9

The narrow lane that runs from Tarrant Gunville to the ominously named and very haunted Bloody Shard Gate.

Tarrant Gunville

Distance:	**6 miles**
Ghostly Rating:	* *
Route:	**Tarrant Gunville - Chettle - Tarrant Gunville**
Map:	**OS Explorer 118**
Start/ Parking:	**Tarrant Gunville High Street**
Public Transport:	**Tarrant Gunville is served by an infrequent bus service from Blandford Forum.**
Conditions:	**A gentle walk over predominantly good surfaces with no stiles or awkward gates.**
Refreshments:	**There is not much on offer in the course of this walk, so it might be best to bring a packed meal and some drink.**

The area around Tarrant Gunville is peaceful and gentle, but it was not always so. The ghosts here are reminders of violent and bloody days in years gone by. The walk takes the visitor through two truly delightful villages and past one of the most picturesque churches in Dorset. There are no steep hills and the route travels mostly over surfaced lanes, though one stretch of bridleway can be sticky after rain.

The Walk

1) Park in the High Street at Tarrant Gunville. The road is narrow in places, so be careful to ensure that your parked vehicle does not obstruct other road users.

2) Walk north out of Tarrant Gunville to where a lane turns off to the right signposted to Bussey Stool. Follow this narrow lane between tall hedges as it climbs along a valley to pass over two crossroads. Beyond the second crossroads the surface becomes gravel and in wet weather has frequent and deep puddles filling the potholes. The track comes to an end as it passes through a gate and runs out in a field.

This is the notorious, and very haunted, Bloody Shard Gate. Back in the late 18th century a notorious and vicious gang of poachers operated

The Bloody Shard Gate, scene of a violent fight between local gamekeepers and an organised gang of poachers.

around this area of Dorset, known as Cranborne Chase. These were not local farmhands who bagged the odd rabbit or pheasant for their family pot. They were organised, violent men who killed and stole large numbers of deer to sell for cash at the London meat markets. They did not care who got hurt or what injuries they inflicted, just so long as they got away with prime meat. The gang intimidated locals into silence and beat gamekeepers close to death. It was a bad time to be honest in the village of Tarrant Gunville. Although just about everyone in the area knew that the gang was led by a retired sergeant of dragoons named Blandford from the village of Pimperne, nobody could be found to testify against him and his gang.

So the local landowners and gamekeepers came up with a plan. They arranged for a tip off to be given to the gang that a particularly fine herd of deer were lurking around Farnham Woods. Knowing that the best access was through the gate now known as Bloody Shard, the gamekeepers lay in wait, armed and equipped with leg irons and handcuffs. Right on cue Sergeant Blandford and his poachers came into sight, dragging a pair of fine deer carcasses behind them.

A dragoon of the 18th century. It was a retired dragoon sergeant who was the cause of the violent fight at Bloody Shard Gate.

The gamekeepers pounced, determined to rid the area of the gang of poachers once and for all. It was, by all accounts, a vicious fight. One keeper had three ribs broken and a second, famous as the finest boxer in the county, had his leg broken. In the course of the fighting Sergeant Blandford had his right hand sliced clean off by a gamekeeper's sword. The gang were eventually overpowered and sent to Dorchester for trial.

Which left the gamekeepers with the problem of what to do with the severed hand. After some discussion they took it to the vicar at Pimperne and had it buried in the churchyard. The poachers were transported for up to seven years apiece to the new colony in what is now Australia. Some years later Blandford returned to England, set up a shop in London and by all accounts lived a respectable life until his death.

And it was then that the ghosts began to walk – or in one case to crawl. Both the dead man and his severed hand returned to the scene of the fight where they were separated. The man wanders around the area, head bent to scan the ground. The severed hand drags itself around the ground as if trying to be noticed. To date the two have not been seen together. Perhaps if the hand finds the man, or the man finds the hand, the ghosts will vanish forever.

3) From Bloody Shard Gate, take the bridleway which heads off southeast. The route leaves Bloody Shard Gate between two metal posts and is identified by a plastic disc carrying the blue arrow which Dorset County Council erects to identify its public rights of way. The bridleway runs with a wood to its left, though some scrub borders it to the right. After passing Greenclose Farm, the bridleway runs across open fields before reaching a second wood and this time passing on the left side of the wood. Beyond the wood, the bridleway runs across another field, dotted with mature trees.

4) Where the main track turns right to pass through a hedge and climb towards a barn, this walk bears left. Again following the Dorset County Council blue arrows, it passes through a gap in a hedge to continue more or less straight on in the direction it had been following. The walk now runs along the right hand edge of a field. At the end of the hedge there is a gap on the right, followed by a gateway, though the open gate is overgrown by brambles and quite unable to move. This gateway gives on to a broad surfaced track which runs uphill to a gate which does work. Beyond this gate is a surfaced lane.

5) Go straight on along this lane as it runs between hedges and down into the village of Chettle. Pass the hotel and restaurant on the right.

6) Take a turning on the right signposted to Chettle House. At the church take the right hand fork in the lane. The church is one of the prettiest in Dorset and will more than repay the time taken to pause here on the walk. Passing on, the lane has the entrance to Chettle House on the left. Chettle House is a fine old mansion that has some of the loveliest gardens in Dorset. It is open during the summer, and the fine gardens in the spring and autumn as well. Again, it is worth paying a visit.

7) Just beyond Chettle House, the lane ends confusingly in three gates. The walk goes through the central gate, along a track marked with one of Dorset County Council's red arrows, indicating a public byway. The byway goes straight ahead, passing a wood on the right, and ends at a T-junction.

8) Turn left along a new byway which crosses open country before curving in a gentle arc through woodland. The byway then runs straight down a modest hill to reach a surfaced lane beside a postbox.

9) Turn right. This lane runs back towards Tarrant Gunville, but before it reaches the village the lane passes an ornate set of gates on the right with impressive stone pillars, balustrades and finials.

These are the mighty gates to Eastbury House. This magnificent mansion is a private house and not open to the public, but that is no great problem as it is the gates that are haunted. The house was begun by the fabulously wealthy and aristocratic George Dodington in 1718. Just two years later, however, Dodington died childless and left his vast wealth to a remote relative named George Bubb. This son of a Weymouth shopkeeper was just 29 years old. The sudden wealth seems

The charming little church at Chettle.

A cow and her calf, just one of several sculptures that adorn the hedgerows around Chettle.

to have gone to his head. He moved into a cottage in the grounds of Eastbury and at once decided that his benefactor's plans were not grand enough. Young George, who had now changed his name to Dodington, employed the most prestigious architect of his day, Vanburgh, to complete the house in the grandest style possible. Only Blenheim and Castle Howard were to be larger. Young George wanted to out do even the King of England. The house cost a staggering £140,000 at a time when most workers would earn only a few pounds each year.

But even this grand house was not enough for George Bubb Dodington. Now thirsting after a career in public life he bought himself a rotten seat in Parliament - such things being possible before the Great Reform Act of 1832. For years Dodington threw himself into London life and national politics, but he still used his grand mansion for weekend parties of glittering sophistication.

What Dodington did not know was that his estate manager, William Doggett, was not only spectacularly clever but was also spectacularly dishonest. While Dodington was in London, Doggett was systematically siphoning off his wealth. Because Dodington always sent word in advance when he was coming down from London with friends, Doggett had time to complete the books fraudulently to make everything appear in order.

Then, one fateful day in the later 1740s, Dodington came home unannounced. The evidence of Doggett's misdeeds was clear to see. Doggett shot himself. The financial damage done to the estate was immense. Some years later much of the house had to be taken down as its upkeep was no longer possible. The house as it stands today is but a shadow of its former glory.

A few weeks after he killed himself, Doggett returned in spectral form and shot himself again. Then his phantom walked calmly down to the magnificent gates. There the ghost stood waiting. In time a black coach came up the lane from the south and pulled up in front of the waiting figure. The ghost climbed on board the coach and closed the door behind him. At that moment the coachman threw back his cloak to reveal his pointed tail, cloven hooves and horned head. Laughing manically, the Devil whipped the horses into a frenzy and galloped off with his new prize.

On occasional nights ever since the ghost of Doggett has been seen lurking around by the gates. He wears fashionable clothes from the mid-18th century and his knee breeches are tied up with yellow silk ribbons. For some reason more than one witness has mentioned the yellow ribbons. Perhaps they are noticeable in the pale moonlight in which the ghost is most often seen.

Those who see the ghost of Doggett by the gates tend not to linger to watch. Nobody wants to meet the Devil and his coach of doom.

From the gates of Eastbury House continue north along the lane to reach Tarrant Gunville High Street.

The grand gates to Eastbury House, scene of a haunting that prompts most locals to hurry by after dark.

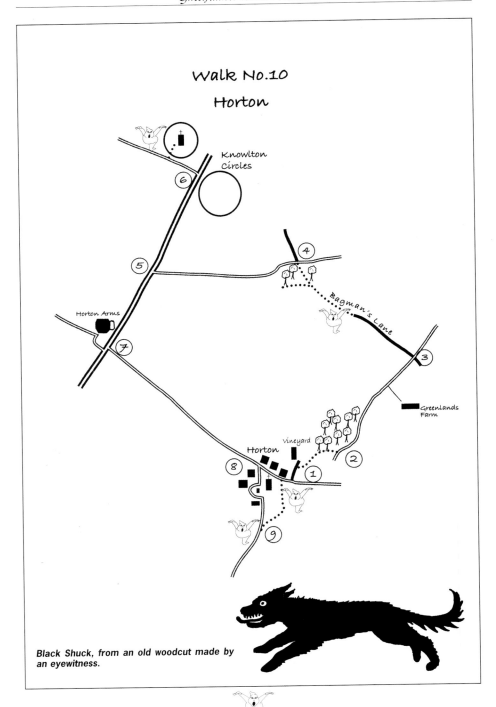

Walk No.10

Horton

Knowlton Circles

Horton Arms

Bagman's Lane

Greenlands Farm

Vineyard

Horton

Black Shuck, from an old woodcut made by an eyewitness.

Horton

Distance:	**6.5 miles**
Ghostly Rating:	**★ ★ ★ ★**
Route:	**Horton - Knowlton - Horton**
Map:	**OS Explorer 118**
Start/ Parking:	**Horton High Street**
Public Transport:	**Horton is linked by an infrequent bus service to Wimborne.**
Conditions:	**A gentle walk over good surfaces with no stiles or awkward gates.**
Refreshments:	**There is a fine selection of bar meals and ales available at the Horton Inn.**

This is an atmospheric area. The ghosts here are as old as any in England and one of them is dangerous as well. The landmarks along the walk range from the truly ancient to the modern and from the enigmatic to the frivolous. Much of this walk is along surfaced lanes, but for the most part these are quiet and see little traffic. Only the B3078 has much in the way of traffic to bother the walker, but generous grass verges give plenty of room to walk.

The Walk

1) Park in the High Street at Horton. There is a layby at the eastern end of the High Street near a prominent phone box.

From the layby walk up the driveway signposted to the vineyard. After about 100 yards the imposing gates of the vineyard close off the drive, and a wide footpath veers off to the right. Follow this path as it runs between two fences across a field. At the top of a slight slope the path enters woodland, through which it runs a short distance before emerging on to a lane.

2) Turn left along this lane. Follow the lane past houses, ignoring a signpost for a footpath on the left and continuing on past an imposing entrance to Greenlands Farm on the right. A short distance further on, a driveway on the right faces a broad gravel track on the left.

Bagman's Lane, just north of Horton, is home to a terrifying phantom which can bring death and disaster in its wake.

3) Turn left down this gravel track.

This track is Bagmans Lane. It has recently been designated as a byway open to all traffic and the surface has been improved, and should soon see further work. It is here that the walker should tread carefully, for this is the haunt of a terrifying and dangerous phantom. The spectre appears in the shape of a truly enormous black dog with shaggy hair and large eyes that glow with a form of inner fire as if lit by glowing coals. The dog lollops along from a distance as if running with a purpose. And a purpose it has – a most sinister one. It is looking for those humans marked for death. If it passes you by without glancing at you, count yourself lucky. But if it stops and growls, then you would be well advised to get your affairs in order and visit the nearest church in search of Divine forgiveness. Your time is nigh!

This black dog is a familiar phantom which is seen in several places across Dorset and, indeed, England. Some believe it is a relic of pre-Christian days. The black dog is seen often near ancient holy sites, and as we shall see, Bagman's Lane is close to one of these. Perhaps this Black Shuck, as the dog is known, is some ancient god or demon who has survived the Christian conquest of these islands.

After a few hundred yards the gravel surface runs out and Bagman's Lane continues as an earthen path running between high hedges and overhanging trees. This stretch of the road is most atmospheric and it is here that the great black dog is said to be seen most frequently. At a fork in the path, take what appears to be the right hand fork but does in fact run straight on.

4) This emerges on to a lane where another track runs straight on. Turn left along the lane. After a short distance a sweeping view opens up to the right. If you look carefully you should see a stone church about a mile away. This is Knowlton to which the walk is going.

The ruined church of Knowlton, centre of several legends as well as an ancient haunting.

The lane south of Horton which is frequented by a friendly and playful phantom.

5) At the end of the lane, turn right on to the B3078. After the road passes some farm buildings, a lane turns off to the left.

6) Turn down this lane. A gate on the right after 100 yards or so gives access to Knowlton Church.

This church is ruined, having stood roofless and windowless for generations. The church stands in the centre of a circular earthwork which has a steep bank standing outside a deep ditch. This is a henge and it dates back around 4,000 years to the Neolithic period. Like the more famous Stonehenge, Knowlton Henge was a centre of worship for our remote ancestors. It lacked the standing stones of Stonehenge, but may have had upright wooden posts instead. No doubt the church was built here to put a definitive Christian stamp on a centre of the old religion.

This is a peaceful and restful place where you may care to relax at this stage of the walk. It is also haunted. Most locals know the place is haunted, but few know what by. One local woman declared that the phantom was that of a tall man dressed in a long cloak. This is interesting. Some miles to the north in Wiltshire is a Neolithic burial chamber of West Kennet, which is haunted by a tall man in a white cloak accompanied by a large dog. Are these phantoms connected to the old religion? Is the tall man of Knowlton linked to the dangerous dog of Bagman's Lane? If so, it would tie the Neolithic Knowlton to the same aged ruins at West Kennet. It is a mystery.

Equally mysterious is what happened to the church bells. One was taken to Sturminster Marshall and a second to Shapwick. The third, the largest and the one with the most beautiful ring, was left at Knowlton. Although the village the church served faded away and the church fell into ruins, the bell remained. Then, one day many generations ago, a group

Sheep graze peacefully unaware of the history of their pasture and of the ghosts that are rumoured to walk there.

of local roughs decided to steal the bell, ship it to France and sell it. Everything was arranged, a cart was brought to the abandoned church and a boat waited at Swanage. Unfortunately for the would-be robbers, a passing traveller saw them at work and raised the alarm. By the time help arrived, the roughs were well away, whipping their horses to carry the bell away. They got as far as Sturminster Newton when the hurrying cart struck the parapet of the bridge, overturned and threw the bell into the River Stour.

There the bell lay for some days before ropes and horses could be organised to pull it out. But no matter how hard the local men tried, nor how often they harnessed their horses, something always went wrong. Either the ropes broke, or the horses refused to move, or the harness slipped. And so the bell remained in the Stour where, when flood waters rage down the stream, it can be heard tolling as it tumbles about.

This is an interesting legend and may take us back to the old religion once again. Dorset was the home territory of the Durotiges, one of the more tenacious of the pre-Roman Celtic tribes. They fought ferociously against the Romans and, four centuries later, equally hard against the invading English. The Stour was one of their sacred rivers, and demanded that sacrifices be hurled into the waters at regular intervals.

Is the old story about the bells of Knowlton some dim memory of a struggle between the Christian church with its bells and the old gods with their sacred rivers? Perhaps.

From Knowlton, return back along the B3078 to pass the lane by which you joined it. 200 yards further on a lane turns off left opposite the Horton Inn.

7) Stop for a drink and a meal if you like, then turn left down the lane signposted to Horton.

This lane drops down a hill as it enters the village.

8) A lane turns off right signposted to Chalbury Common in the centre of the village. Follow this road. Just beyond the spot where it turns sharp right and leaves the village the lane starts to climb a gentle slope.

This stretch of road is haunted by a playful spectre. This is the phantom of a small boy, aged about 10 years old and dressed in clothes which seem to date him to the 17th century. He runs around playing games, darting in front of cars and generally enjoying himself. Nobody knows who he is nor why he haunts this particular stretch of road. At the top of the slope stands the impressive bulk of Horton Tower. This is merely a folly built for the idle pleasure of the local gentry, but it is an easy landmark.

9) As the lane climbs the slight hill, a footpath leaves to the left beside the driveway to a house called The Oaks. The path cuts back towards the village and runs across an open field to a stile visible some 400 yards distant. Once across the stile you find yourself in a grassy field which has many strange bumps and mounds.

This field is haunted by a most gentle spirit. That of a nun. She walks quietly, with head bowed and arms folded in contemplation. This ghost is not seen often and, even then, usually in the early morning. The mounds and dips give a clue to the reason for this ghost. This is the site of a medieval Abbey which was dissolved by Henry VIII in the mid-16th century. The wealth was stripped out together with any valuable building materials, leaving just piles of rubble behind. In the intervening centuries these have become grassed over to become pasture for the sheep of Horton. Now only the ghostly nun seems to remember what this field once was.

Cross the field towards the gate visible in the far left hand corner. This gate opens on to the High Street. The driveway to the Vineyard is just 30 yards to the right.

The Horton Nun.

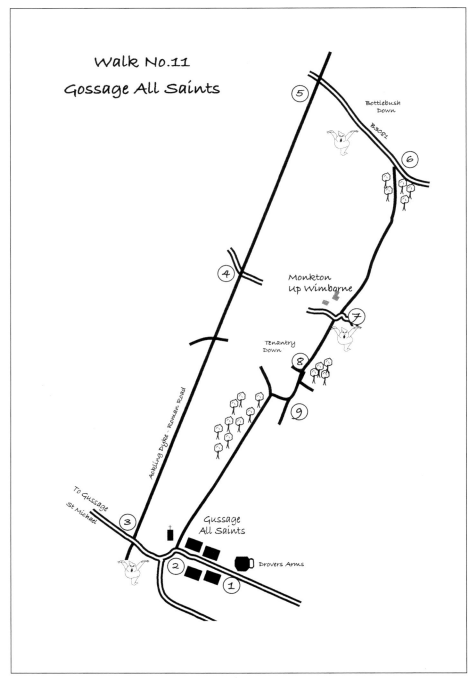

Walk No.11

Gossage All Saints

Gussage All Saints

Distance:	**7.5 miles**
Ghostly Rating:	*** * ***
Route:	**Gussage All Saints - Ackling Dyke - Bottlebush Down - Monkton Up Wimborne - Gussage All Saints**
Map:	**OS Explorer 118**
Start/ Parking:	**Gussage All Saints**
Public Transport:	**Gussage All Saints is linked by an infrequent bus service to Blandford Forum.**
Conditions:	**A lengthy but gentle walk on good surfaces which takes the walker over some of the oldest pathways in Britain.**
Refreshments:	**This is largely open country devoid of human habitation of any kind. However, just off the walk route in Gussage All Saints is the welcoming Drovers Inn which offers a fine selection of pub fare.**

This is an area of gentle, rolling hills which offers nothing in the way of strenuous climbing. But the land is quite high and there are occasional and spectacular views across surrounding countryside. The walk takes you through 4,000 years of history, and includes what is possibly the oldest ghost in England - it is certainly the oldest phantom still lurking in Dorset.

The Walk

1) Park in Gussage All Saints. If you are intending to refresh yourself at the Drovers Inn, you are welcome to use their car park. Otherwise park towards the northern end of the village near the church.

2) Follow the village high street as it turns sharp left by the church, then sharp right to leave the village in a northwesterly direction towards Gussage St Michael.

This stretch of road, and other lanes in the area, is haunted by an open carriage drawn by a smart pair of black horses. Sitting in the carriage is an exquisitely dressed Restoration gentleman. This is the first Lord Shaftesbury who owned lands hereabouts. This is not the philanthropist after whom Shaftesbury Avenue in London was named, but an altogether more sinister ancestor of his.

The modern recycling bins which mark the point where the old Roman road crosses the modern lane just west of Gussage All Saints.

Born the humble Anthony Cooper, Shaftesbury led an adventurous life. He inherited a comfortable estate in Dorset, but was not happy with a quiet country life. His chance came in the Civil War of the 1640s. Like most other Dorset gentry, Cooper joined the Royalist cause. After 10 months, however, Cooper saw the way the wind was blowing and promptly changed sides to become a vocal supporter of Oliver Cromwell. Other Parliamentarians did not trust Cooper, believing his support had more to do with the opportunities for self enrichment than any devotion to Parliament. As soon as Cromwell died, his generals threw Cooper into prison. The wily Cooper talked his way out of prison, however, and at once changed sides again by sailing to France to join the exiled King Charles II. When Charles returned to England, Cooper was once again in high favour. It was Charles who ennobled Cooper as the Earl of Shaftesbury.

But Shaftesbury could not stick to a single cause for long. Seeing that Charles was unlikely to father a legitimate heir, Shaftesbury realised that the king's brother James would be the next monarch. However, Shaftesbury's well-known Protestantism made him unpopular with the Catholic James, who promised to deprive him of his offices as soon as possible. Shaftesbury turned to plotting once again. This time his schemes involved the dashing, handsome and safely Protestant Duke of Monmouth, a bastard son of Charles. Shaftesbury began spreading rumours that Charles had secretly married Monmouth's mother before the boy was born. The mother was safely dead and could not deny the rumours. Charles denied the allegation, but Shaftesbury's agents ensured the rumours spread even wider.

In 1683 King Charles finally tired of Shaftesbury and sent him into exile. After Charles died, Monmouth led a rebellion that was to fail in tragic circumstances and leave its ghostly mark in Dorset at Lyme Regis and Dorchester. Before Monmouth went to the block, Shaftesbury had changed sides yet again, this time finally. He had died and gone to join his God.

But his ghost came back to his ancestral acres around Gussage All Saints. Who knows what wily, twisted plans the artful Shaftesbury is hatching as he rides in spectral fashion around the lanes of Dorset. Whatever his plots may be, he keeps them to himself.

3) About 200 yards outside the village the lane is crossed by a bridleway. The route to the right is signposted as a footpath to Harley Down. This junction is clearly recognisable as the village recycling bank is located here, with the usual large and brightly coloured plastic containers for old bottles and the like. Turn right off the lane onto the bridlepath towards Harley Down.

This bridleway is, in fact, the Ackling Way – a Roman road built to run from Salisbury to Dorchester. Like most Roman roads, this is broad, smooth and above all straight. This particular example climbs the gentle slope out of the valley and runs along the high ground in a dead straight line to the northeast. Simply follow this path straight ahead, ignoring paths or tracks to either side.

4) After almost two miles the Ackling Way crosses a modern surfaced lane. Go straight across and continue along the Roman Road.

5) After another mile or so the walk meets a more substantial modern road, the B3081. This high and often windswept ground is known as Bottlebush Down. Turn right and walk along this road until you find a prehistoric burial mound close by the road in a field on the right.

It is this burial mound which forms the centre of perhaps the oldest haunting in Britain. Galloping over the grassy downs towards this barrow rides a ferocious warrior. He rides without a saddle and brandishes over his head a long sword. The man seems to be showing off his martial valour for all to see. He appears near the wood known as Squirrel's Corner and gallops northwest over the downs towards the barrow.

As he rides the warrior crosses an ancient and enigmatic earthwork known to modern archaeologists as a cursus. This cursus consists of a bank of earth dug out of a ditch which runs alongside it. The bank and ditch runs across the land for several miles, then bends in a tight semicircle to return across the land just a few yards south of, and parallel to, the first ditch. What the purpose of these features was is unknown, but there are several in southern Britain. One of them runs across Salisbury Plain near Stonehenge.

In the 1930s an archaeologist who was studying this cursus was both surprised and amazed to see the phantom horseman galloping towards him. Unlike most others who have seen this ghost, the archaeologist was in a position to give an expert appraisal of the phantom. The sword he wielded and the jewellery he wore placed this man unquestionably in the Bronze Age. This made him around 3,500 years old, and about the same age as the cursus and the barrow.

It has been suggested that, since he vanishes beside the barrow, the ghostly warrior might be the man buried within. Certainly these barrows were the burial places of rulers, priests and powerful men. Those that have been excavated usually reveal a skeleton accompanied by swords, jewels and gold. Is the ghost retracing the route of his funeral procession, or is he merely showing off his vigour and valour to the modern world? Whatever his purpose he is pursuing it with a dedication that reaches across the millennia.

6) Just after the road enters woodland, a metal gate opens through the fence on the right hand side. Go through this gate and walk straight on, following Dorset County Council's blue arrow indicating a bridleway. The path through the trees soon broadens and, where it emerges from the

The ancient barrow on Bottlebush Down which is haunted by the oldest ghost in Dorset.

A Bronze Age warrior wearing equipment almost identical to that worn by the ghostly horseman of Bottlebush Down.

woods, becomes a wide grassy track between high hedges. This is the old Monkton Drove, one of many drover routes that run across Britain. The drovers were the men who drove cattle or sheep from the lands where they were raised to the towns and cities where they could be sold. Usually livestock were raised on poor upland country where crops would not grow. The main market for them was in the lowland towns. Before the days of rail or motorised road traffic, the only realistic way to get the meat from hill to market was on the hoof. Thus the drovers walked the countryside, pushing their herds from watering hole to grazing land on the weeks-long journey to market.

7) The drove track winds its way southwest over the rolling hills for over a mile until it meets a narrow, surfaced lane. Turn right. After about 100 yards a bridleway turns left, opposite a post box and the entrance to Manor Farm. The small group of houses in front of you is the hamlet of Monkton Up Wimborne. The name is descriptive for this little place is upstream along the Allen from Wimborne St Giles. It takes its name of Monkton from the fact that in medieval times there was a tiny chapel here attended by a lone monk. The chapel stood in the field behind the postbox, but no trace of it remains above ground today.

Some people have reported seeing a shifting, mysterious something on this stretch of road. One person said it was a lady dressed in grey, a second that it was a man dressed in a grey cloak. This may indicate that the phantom is one of the long vanished monks who once served at this remote little chapel. On the other hand, this is a damp little hollow which is given to mists and vapours. The strange, shapeless grey figure may be nothing more than a wisp of mist.

Take the bridleway opposite the post box. This is a continuation of the drove road, but here is narrower and more sheltered by trees. It climbs uphill on to the high ground known as Tenantry Down.

8) Ignore the gravel track that comes in from the right, then

The gentle slope of the cursus, a mysterious prehistoric earthwork, close to which the ancient phantom appears before galloping towards the burial

leaves to the left 100 yards further on, but continue straight on.

9) Where a wooden barrier blocks the bridleway, turn right down a wide gravel track which runs down into the valley and then turns left beside the woodland on the opposite slope. Follow this broad gravel track as it runs along the valley. Ignore side paths and surfaced tracks, but continue straight on round the shoulder of the hill running down from the left. As the path drops down beyond this hill it passes a couple of houses before merging back into the High Street of Gussage All Saints beside the church and war memorial.

The broad, grassy drovers' track that runs over the downs north of Tarrant Gunville.

Monkton Up Wimborne was home to a succession of medieval hermits, one of whom may return in spectral form.

The damp hollow where a misty "something" has been reported. Is it a ghost, or a swirling patch of mist?

Walk No.12
Beaminster

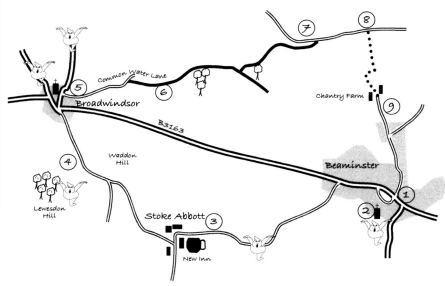

Common Water Lane

5 Broadwindsor 6

7 8

Chantry Farm

9

B3163

Waddon Hill

4

Beaminster

Lewesdon Hill

Stoke Abbott 3

1

2

New Inn

The quiet lane leading to Stoke Abbott, the peace of which is sometimes shattered by a dramatic ghostly apparition.

Beaminster

Distance:	**8 miles**
Ghostly Rating:	* * * * *
Route:	**Beaminster - Stoke Abbott - Broadwindsor - Beaminster**
Map:	**OS Explorer 116**
Start/ Parking:	**Beaminster Market Square**
Public Transport:	**Beaminster is served by an hourly bus service from Bridport, while a less frequent route links it to the railway station at Crewkerne.**
Conditions:	**A long walk with steep slopes and some muddy ground, but it offers spectacular views and rewarding scenery.**
Refreshments:	**Beaminster is a busy, if small, town which has a variety of pubs, cafes and restaurants. Both Stoke Abbott and Broadwindsor offer pub food, though opening times vary.**

The phantoms of the land around Beaminster are a varied group, and the scenery is equally diverse. There are narrow, quiet lanes, wide open hillsides offering sweeping views and dense woodland rich in wildlife. The more challenging sections of this walk can be bypassed by those who prefer an easier outing, but this short cut also misses out the finest views and most impressive scenery. Beaminster itself is an engaging little town with a surprisingly diverse range of shops to visit. There are pubs and restaurants in plenty. All in all, Beaminster is a lively little place that makes a good centre for the surrounding countryside and a welcoming place to halt awhile.

The Walk

1) Park in Beaminster, if possible in the Market Square but if this small area is full use the nearby car park. Leave the Market Square by way of Church Street. At the bottom of Church Street is the parish Church of St Mary's with its recently restored 15th century tower.

It was just at this church that a murder most foul was unmasked on 27 June 1728. The victim was a schoolboy named John Daniel. He had died around six weeks before from what appeared to have been a fit. Then his ghost was seen by a group of his fellow shoolboys sitting beside a phantom coffin in the nave of the church. When the boys approached him, the ghost looked up mournfully as if to say something, but then vanished. The boys included

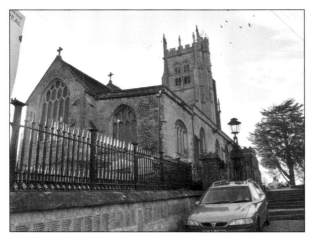

The Church at Beaminster, centre of a haunting that led to official investigations.

one who had moved to the village just a week earlier and had never met the deceased John Daniel, but he could give an accurate description of the dead boy merely by seeing the ghost.

Colonel Broadrepp, the local Justice of the Peace, heard about the sighting and questioned the boys closely. Believing that the appearance of the ghost signified something, but not sure what, Broadrepp ordered the corpse to be exhumed. Although the body had begun to decompose, there was enough evidence of foul play to persuade Broadrepp to investigate. He found that the coroner had been drunk at the hearing and had ignored a witness who claimed that young Daniel had told her he was in fear of his life. Suspicion centred on Daniel's stepmother Elizabeth Daniel, but there was no real evidence that she had killed the boy. Local opinion was firmly against her, however, and she had to leave Beaminster. In contrast, the ghost of poor young John has never left Beaminster. He is seen from time to time sitting quietly in the church, perhaps forever waiting for justice to be done.

2) Walk past the church, keeping the churchyard on the left. Where the road bends right, follow it to a main road. Turn left and, after about 200 yards, left again, up a hill. This is the lane that leads to Stoke Abbott.

This lane is haunted. Local talk has it that the coach and four which races down this narrow, twisting lane belongs to the Wicked Squire. Which squire this might be and why he is considered wicked is unclear. Everyone is very definite, however, that it is best to stay out of his way. Only bad luck and ill fortune will come to those who hinder this phantom coach in its headlong rush to Stoke Abbott.

The ancient spring of Stoke Abbott beside a seat that provides a welcome sit-down for passing walkers.

A hill to be avoided: the home of the fairies south of Broadwindsor.

3) The narrow lane twists and turns through open country, sometimes diving into a sunken lane, until it reaches the village of Stoke Abbott. Pass the pub on the left and follow the road as it bends left. On the right is a freshwater spring which emerges through a finely carved stone lion's head which has a small cup attached to it by a chain. A park bench stands nearby, offering a welcome opportunity to sit and relax beneath a spreading oak tree planted to commemorate the coronation of King Edward VII over a century ago. At this tree turn right. Follow this lane, until it ends at a T-junction. Turn right.

4) Where a signed public footpath leaves the road through a gate on the left, next to a house, go to the gate and look south towards a tree-covered hill. This is Lewesdon Hill.

The wooded slopes are home to the little people, but these are not gentle, magical fairies that might be encountered in fairy story books. These are entities with an agenda and a determination all their own. The few who claim to have seen the fairies of Lewesdon Hill report them to be quite beautiful humans, though barely three feet tall. There is something charismatically alluring about the little people, but they should not be crossed on any account. In fact it is probably best to avoid them. They are unpredictable and may take a dislike to a human for no readily obvious reason. Picking the wrong flower can be enough to earn the enmity of the little people for they have an affinity with plants and with the natural world. This may be why they prefer the slopes of Lewesdon Hill. The dense woods are blanketed in bluebells in the spring while summer produces dense undergrowth untroubled by human intervention. Which must suit the little people just fine.

5) Continue on along the lane into Broadwindsor. At the crossroads, bear left along the B3162 towards Drimpton. When you reach the church on the right, pause and look along the road straight ahead of you.

If you arrive at the right time you may see coming towards you with slow, measured tread a funeral procession. This is no ordinary funeral for the horse-drawn hearse, the mourners and the coachman are all phantoms. The black-draped hearse leads the way, with men and women walking two by two behind. The mourners are dressed in uniform black, with the men's top hats dating the procession to some time in the 19th century. As the procession

The Church of Broadwindsor, the destination of a ghostly procession that never quite makes it.

reaches the Church of St John the Baptist, the whole entourage vanishes from sight.

The majority of the church was built in the 19th century, though the tower dates back to the 15th century. Within the church is a small plaque commemorating the fact that on 23 September 1651 the tower hid young King Charles II. At the time Charles was on the run after defeat at the Battle of Worcester. The vengeful forces of Oliver Cromwell were hot on his heels, eager to send him to the scaffold and ensure the future of the English Republic that had been established after the execution of Charles I. Young King Charles is better known for hiding up an oak tree than a church tower, but the ruse was just as successful. The young fugitive escaped detection and finally made his way to safety in Europe to await his recall to the throne after Cromwell's death.

At the church, turn right along the short one-way street, turning left at the T junction at which it ends. Pass the churchyard on the left to reach the junction with Common Water Lane on the right.

The road in front of you runs up a steep hill towards the village of Mosterton. This lane is patrolled by one of Dorset's more terrifying spectres: Black Shuck. This spirit takes the form of a gigantic black hound with shaggy hair and glowing red eyes the size of saucers. This alarming apparition is enough to strike fear into any heart just by its sheer size and ferocious looks. But its true horror lies in the fact that this hound is said to foretell death to the person who sees it or to a member of their family. The best plan, it is said, is to leap into the hedgerows beside the road if Black Shuck is seen approaching, and hide. If the dog passes by without giving you a glance you have escaped bad luck, but if it looks at you then misfortune will surely follow.

This is the last phantom on this walk and there is now a choice of routes to return to Beaminster.

To use the short route, return to the crossroads and turn left along the road signposted to Beaminster. This is the B3163 which runs directly to Beaminster offering firm walking with a minimum of hills. It does, however, miss out some of the finest views in Dorset.

6) To continue on the longer, more scenic walk. Turn right into Common Water Lane. Follow this lane downhill to a fork. Take the right hand fork between two blue metal posts on to an unsurfaced bridleway past an overgrown pond on the left. This bridleway climbs gently then passes a wood before rising steeply to a hill summit. The path runs along a ridge known as Horn Hill which offers fine views to both north and south.

7) The path emerges on to a surfaced lane between another pair of blue metal posts. Turn right. About 500 yards along this lane the drive to North Buckham Farm is on the left. Here a bridleway to the left is signposted to Mosterton and a bridleway to the right is signposted to Beaminster. Turn right through a gate.

8) Cross the field in front of you to exit through a gate in the fence on the far side. This gate is heavy and difficult to open and close. Head downhill across this field, ignoring the gateway on the right, to leave it through a gate in the bottom righthand corner. This gate is again heavy and tricky to operate. Beyond the gate turn left and skirt downhill along the lefthand edge of the field. Pass through a gate into an open field that appears to have no exit. There is, in fact, a gap in the bramble and gorse thicket on the far side of the field, but it is not visible until you get close to it. Follow the path as it bends to left, then right to avoid a marshy hollow. As you approach the thicket the gap becomes visible. Pass through the gap and walk downhill along a track through the gorse and brambles. Where this track divides, take the left path and climb

The lane north of Broadwindsor where the hedgerows provide the only refuge from a terrifying apparition.

over a stile. Pass through a clump of small trees and cross a stream using a small concrete bridge. Turn left to walk downhill through a group of saplings. Leave the saplings at the base of the hill through a gap in the fence and follow the path downhill to emerge into Chantry Farm farmyard.

9) Exit on the far side and enter a narrow lane that runs downhill. Where this track meets a wider lane, bear right and continue into Beaminster. Stay on this road until it emerges back into the Market Square.

Common Water Lane, which runs from Broadwindsor towards Beaminster, passes through densely wooded hills and offers sweeping views of the Dorset countryside.

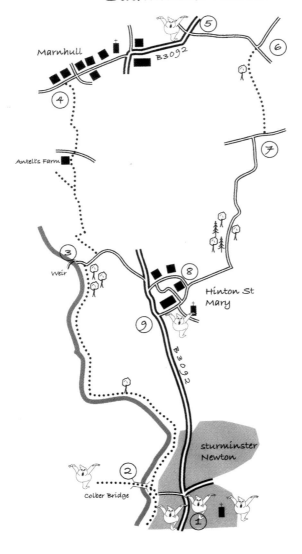

Walk No.13
Sturminster Newton

Sturminster Newton

Distance:	**9 miles**
Ghostly Rating:	* * * * *
Route:	**Sturminster Newton - Marnhull - Hinton St Mary - Sturminster Newton**
Map:	**OS Explorer 129**
Start/ Parking:	**Sturminster Newton**
Public Transport:	**Sturminster Newton is a centre for bus routes to local villages and is served by frequent services from Blandford Forum, Shaftesbury, Sherborne and Dorchester.**
Conditions:	**A long walk which includes the centre of Sturminster Newton, but which mainly runs through the surrounding countryside, including a section along the banks of the River Stour. The river bank can be muddy after rain, but otherwise the going is generally good and there are no demanding hills.**
Refreshments:	**Sturminster Newton has several pubs and a couple of takeaways. Hinton St Mary has a pub which offers bar meals, as does Marnhull.**

Sturminster Newton is the market town that lies at the heart of the beautiful Blackmoor Vale, through which this walk wends its way. The town stands in a loop of the River Stour, from which it gains its name, and boasts a fine medieval bridge over the river to the south of the town. In 1729 the town was almost completely destroyed by a fire which struck after a long, dry spell of weather and leapt hungrily from thatched roof to thatched roof. Only the church and the White Hart Inn survived. The town as it stands today, is largely the creation of the two or three years after the fire. The livestock market which dominated the town for so long is now gone, but a regular market is held on Mondays and Saturdays.

The Walk

1) Park in one of the small car parks in the town centre and make your way to the Market Place. The open triangular space is dominated by the ornate brickwork of the Swan Inn.

This ancient pub is haunted by the phantom of a landlord who lived here some two centuries ago. The old boy was apparently genial and one of the more popular characters in Stur, as

The church at Sturminster Newton provides a historic focal point for this ancient market town.

the town is known to locals. It came as a considerable shock to the town, therefore, when the man was found hanging in the cellar having committed suicide. Why he should have taken his life nobody could explain for the business was thriving and he was not known to have any personal problems. Perhaps some private tragedy had been gnawing at his soul.

Whatever the reason for his tragic death, the Old Boy was soon back walking his inn. He is seen often even today. He tends to frequent the upstairs area of the inn and is particularly fond of the staircase itself. As in life, so in phantom form, the Old Boy appears a genial chap bustling about whatever business it is that keeps him tied to the Swan Inn. He causes no trouble to anyone. Those who see his portly figure bumbling around report no sense of fear. If anything the spectre seems to be welcoming his human visitors.

From the Swan, walk across the Market Place to the White Hart.

This pub has a more enigmatic and less active ghost than that at the Swan. The grey lady walks in the downstairs bar area, but only infrequently. Nobody knows who she is and, if truth be told, she has not been seen in recent years.

From the White Hart, turn left walking along the Market Place. At the end of the Market Place, turn left into The Rows, a narrow lane opposite Station Road on the right. At the end of this lane go through a kissing gate and along the path signposted to Colber Bridge. At the foot of the hill go through a second kissing gate and continue straight on at the cross path to reach the River Stour at Colber Bridge.

2) The fields beyond the bridge are the site of the vanished medieval village of Colber, but it is not the long vanished inhabitants of this village that haunt the area but the 18th century owner of a farm a short distance to the south, now a restaurant, named Plumber Manor.

Back in the days of the 18th century, the squire was a quarrelsome and violent man who it was best to avoid. His only popularity came from the fact that he was an avid huntsman who entertained the local hunt and its followers with great generosity whenever it was his turn to do so. So fierce was the Squire Plumber's temper that he was in the habit of whipping his hounds if they failed to track down a fox for his day's sport.

One day the belligerent squire went too far in handing out a beating and his dogs turned on him. Now it was Squire Plumber's turn to run from the hounds as he had so often forced foxes to run. From the manor the bizarre hunt ran north across these fields until the enraged hounds caught Squire Plumber and tore him to shreds. No trace of the man was

The Swan Inn, home to one of the most active and least troublesome ghosts in Dorset.

The White Hart, with the medieval market cross in the foreground.

The Colber Bridge over the River Stour. The fields beyond are haunted by a veritable pack of ghosts.

to be found. Their grisly revenge taken, the hounds ran on and were seen no more by the good folk of Stur.

The terrible hunt is recreated in phantom fashion across these fields to this day. If you hear the sound of baying hounds, it is said, you should hide yourself in a ditch or up a tree. Who knows when the terrible, bloodthirsty hounds may tire of tracking the ghostly squire and turn on more solid mortals for their sport.

From Colber Bridge, return to the cross path and turn north along the track signposted to Hinton St Mary. This path is part of the Stour Valley Walk. Follow this signed walk along the banks of the River Stour for over a mile to a weir and a footbridge.

3) Turn right up the lane, leaving it after a hundred yards or so to turn left where the signs for the Stour Valley Walk indicate a route through the hedge. Follow the Walk across the fields, past Antell's Farm and into the village of Marnhull.

4) At Marnhull, turn right along the village street, passing the church on your left and joining the B3092 as it heads east towards Todber.

It is along this road that a funeral procession is sometimes seen making its sad way westward. Now this is a most peculiar funeral. In itself, there is nothing particularly strange about the procession. Six men carry a plain coffin on their shoulders as they walk slowly

The signs that indicate the way along the banks of the Stour.

along the road, and a handful of mourners follow. Such funerals were common enough among the less wealthy country folk in days gone by. Only the wealthy could afford a hearse, so family friends were pressed into service to act as pallbearers at most burials.

What is so odd about the ghostly funeral of Marnhull is that it is walking away from the churchyard. The church of Marnhull with its square tower stands beside the B3092 in the heart of the village, yet the ghostly procession moves resolutely out of the village towards the crossroads of Todber. In late Victorian times a plough turned up a number of human bones at Todber. A local gentleman interested in antiquities investigated and declared, though on what evidence he did not record, that the bones were the mass burial of those killed in some ancient battle that was fought hereabouts. No record of any battle has ever been found and some suspect that the grim discovery may have been an old plague pit.

The truth may be learned from the ghostly procession, but nobody has ever had the courage to stop the ghosts and ask them.

5) At a crossroads, turn right along the lane, signposted to Moorside.

6) After half a mile take a bridleway to the right where a lane joins from the left. Follow this bridleway over the fields until it emerges onto a second surfaced lane.

7) Turn right, then quickly left, along Hinton Lane, signposted to Hinton St Mary.

8) As the lane enters the village, bear left towards the church, passing the church on the left and reaching a crossroads with the B3092.

The narrow lane outside Marnhull which is visited by a most morbid apparition.

It was just here that building work in the 1950s unearthed the remains of a sumptuous Roman villa. Lying close below the ground surface was one of the finest mosaics ever to be found in Britain. It was lifted piece by piece with great care and taken to the British Museum where it was the centrepiece of an exhibition in 1963.

The lane at Hinton St Mary where one of Britain's finest Roman mosaics was unearthed, with spectral repercussions the archaeologists cannot have expected.

Soon after the mosaic was removed a shadowy figure began to be seen lurking around the site of the excavation. Dressed in a tunic and walking with slow, aimless steps, the ghost seemed to be focussed on the long-vanished villa. It was believed locally that the excavation had disturbed some ancient spirit which had been resting peacefully here for the past 1,600 years. Some wondered whether the phantom would wreak some dreadful revenge for being disturbed, but nothing dramatic happened. The morose phantom just drifts around the site, perhaps wondering where his sumptuous home has gone to - or perhaps for the ghost the villa remains there and he is enjoying its splendours still.

A Roman in his toga, the formal dress of a gentleman in the days when Britain was ruled by Rome.

9) The walker now has a choice. The quickest return route is directly south along the B3092 to Sturminster Newton. However this is a fairly busy B road. A longer, but more pleasant return, is to turn right along the B3092 for 150 yards to find Marriage Lane leaving to the left at a slight angle. Follow this lane back down to the River Stour and rejoin the Stour Valley Walk along the river bank to return to Sturminster Newton along the outward path.

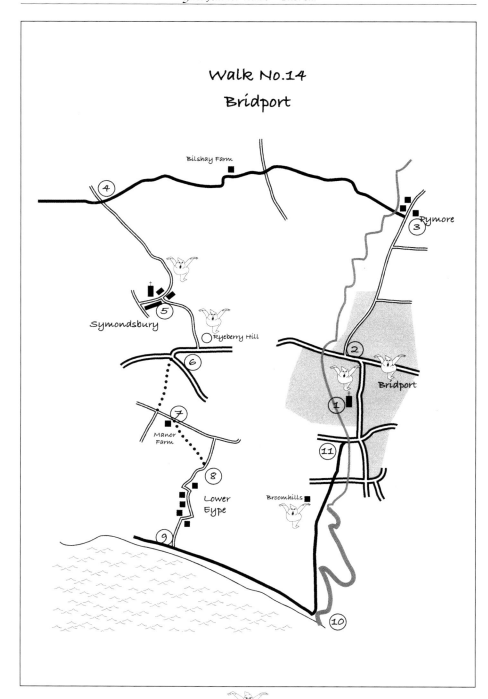

Walk No.14
Bridport

Bilshay Farm

4

Rymore

3

5

Symondsbury

Ryeberry Hill

6

2

Bridport

7

Manor Farm

1

11

8

Lower Eype

Broomhills

9

10

Bridport

Distance:	**9.5 miles**
Ghostly Rating:	★ ★ ★ ★ ★
Route:	**Bridport - Pymore - Symondsbury - Lower Eype - West Bay - Bridport**
Map:	**OS Explorer 116**
Start/ Parking:	**Bridport**
Public Transport:	**Bridport is linked by an hourly bus service to Dorchester and to Lyme Regis, and by less frequent services to other towns.**
Conditions:	**A long walk which covers steep hills and some difficult ground, but which elsewhere covers surfaced lanes and paths.**
Refreshments:	**Bridport is a busy town with a wide variety of pubs, cafes and restaurants. Both Symondsbury and Lower Eype have pubs serving good food.**

This walk takes in stunning coastal scenery, the town centre of Bridport and some spectacular hills. It is, however, both long and, in places, steep and demanding. The supernatural face of the walk is varied and unusual, with many witnesses confirming even the more bizarre phenomena.

The Walk

1) Park in Bridport and walk to the Church off South Street.

This church is the centre of activity by a terrifying beast which is seen at various places in Dorset. This is Black Shuck, a massive black hound with glowing eyes which comes to announce death or misfortune to those who cross its path. This particular manifestation of the Black Shuck is rather untypical in that he does not pace along lanes or run down footpaths. Instead he is reported to sit outside the church and stare balefully at those to whom he is bringing his message of ill fortune. Bizarrely he is said to be invisible to everyone except his victim,

A marker for the Monarch's Trail along much of which the Bridport walk makes its way.

The gate where the Monarch's Way opens on to a lane north of Symondsbury.

others being quite unable to see anything at all even when the gigantic dog is pointed out to them.

From the church walk north along South Street to a T-junction. Look right down East Street to see the old Bull Hotel.

The Bull Hotel saw some bloody action during the ill-fated rebellion of the Duke of Monmouth in 1685. A force of rebels marched on the town in June during the early stages of the rebellion. Some townsmen welcomed the men of the Protestant Duke, but others were more cautious and refused to hand over the stores and weapons the rebels demanded. One of these latter citizens was Wadham Strangeways. He was shot for his troubles and, badly wounded, carried to the Bull where he died.

The room of this gentleman's death has long been reported to be haunted. Many people feel rather uneasy for no apparent reason in this room, now reserved for functions but used occasionally as a restaurant. Only a few actually see the ghost of the long dead victim of rebellion. He stands silently staring out of a window, now blocked up, which then gave a good view of the street outside and of the milling rebel troops who had killed him.

2) Turn left along West Street, then second right into Victoria Grove. Follow this lane for a mile, ignoring two turnings to the right.

3) Just before the Pymore Factory turn left on to the Monarch's Way, a well signposted long-distance walk which at this point is a clear bridleway. Follow the Monarch's Way over the hills, across a lane and past Bilshay Farm until it crosses a second lane.

4) Where the path emerges on to a surfaced lane, turn left downhill.

Just before this lane enters the village of Symondsbury it is haunted by the phantom of a young girl, perhaps ten years of age, who weeps inconsolably as she walks towards the village. More than one person has thought this to be a girl on her way to the village school and tried to offer reassurance. The phantom vanishes if approached so nobody has ever been able to discover who she is nor why she weeps in such an upsetting fashion.

The lane on the outskirts of Symondsbury where more than one person has mistaken the playful spectre for a real person.

5) At the church, turn left, keeping the school on your right. This road leads down

The conical hill near Symondsbury where some distinctly unfriendly little people are said to have their home.

to the conical-shaped Ryeberry Hill on the left, with steep-sided Sloes Hill on the right.

These two conical hills are distinctive landmarks for this region of Dorset and can be seen from a distance of many miles. They are said to be the homes of a tribe of the little people who delight in leading astray human children, especially girls. Given half a chance the beautiful fairies will play music of a haunting and mesmeric quality that lures the unwary child to these hills. Once there, the children are led to a mysterious door in the side of the hill and enticed within.

Once in the fairy land the children are kept as slaves and fed on a special food which ensures they forget all about their families and believe that they are living in a palace of unsurpassed beauty and elegance. The very few children who have escaped say that they have at some point eaten of the food reserved for the fairy children. At once the spell is broken. Not only do they recall their families, but they can see the dingy caves within the hills for the damp subterranean chambers that they really are. These children lose no time at all fleeing back to their human homes. Without exception, however, they find that they have been away much longer than they thought. While they themselves think they have been away a mere few days, they find that in reality months or even years have passed by. Bizarrely the missing children have not aged at all.

The little people are not always the friendly fairies of story books. Those living south of Symondsbury are definitely best avoided.

6) Beyond the pair of hills is a T-junction. Turn right and follow this road down to a second T-junction, this time with the A35. Straight across the main road is a gateway beside a milestone. Pass through this gate and walk straight across the field, leaving via a stile to cross a second field before climbing steeply to pass through a gate and reach a narrow lane.

7) Turn left and walk along this narrow lane to the entrance to Manor Farm on the right.

Turn right along the signposted public footpath, striking straight across a field, crossing into a second field and keeping to the right side of this field.

8) Climb over a stile and scramble down into a sunken lane. Turn right and follow this narrow lane steeply downhill into the village of Lower Eype. Continue along the lane until it reaches the sea at a small car park.

9) Exit the car park down the flight of steps on the left and cross the Eype stream by a small wooden bridge.

If you glance to the left as you cross the bridge you see a Second World War machine gun pill box half hidden in the undergrowth. Defensive posts such as this were scattered all along the south coast during the summer of 1940 to guard against German raids and invasion. These isolated posts were manned by just a few men, sometimes from the Home Guard. If Germans landed, the defenders had orders to send off a runner to alert the nearest regular army command while those who remained held off the Germans as long as possible. Fortunately, the Germans never came.

Follow the path up the steps across the bridge to join the South West Coastal Path.

10) At the mouth of the River Brit the South West Coast Path continues east over a bridge. Ignore the bridge and head up the banks of the river along the Monarch's Way which was followed earlier in the walk. Where the path crosses a main road, glance to your left to see Broomhills Farm.

This farm is over four centuries old and for at least half that time has been home to the Cloaked Lady. This phantom, as her name suggests, is a lady wearing a long cloak which has a hood. She is seen most often beside the driveway which runs from the farmhouse to

The beach at Eype.

the A35. Now that the old farm caters for the tourist trade, she is seen more often. Only on very rare occasions does the lady venture into the house itself, preferring the fresh sea air that wafts up from the English Channel to the south.

11) Continue along the Monarch's Way until it enters Bridport over a weir. Having crossed the weir, turn left off the path to walk up South Street and so return back to the Church.

The Grey Lady of Broomhills.

About the Author

Rupert Matthews has been a ghosthunter for years, tracking down the weird and the supernatural across Britain. He is the author of more than a dozen books on the subject and writes regular columns in several local newspapers. As a keen walker, Rupert is ideally qualified to write a guide to haunted walks in Dorset. Rupert is married with one child. www.rupertmatthews.com.

The author and his family on the haunted beach at Lulworth.